Confessions of a NEW YORK Girl that DARED to Dream

Maralyn Burae

Confessions of a NEW YORK Girl that DARED to Dream. Copyright 2022 by Maralyn Burae. All rights reserved. No part of this publication may be reproduced, distributed, or transmitted in any form or by any means, including photocopying, recording, or other electronic or mechanical methods, without the prior written permission of the publisher, except in the case of brief quotations embodied in critical reviews and certain other noncommercial uses permitted by copyright law.

For permission requests, write to the publisher, addressed "Attention: Permissions Coordinator," 205 N. Michigan Avenue, Suite #810, Chicago, IL 60601. 13th & Joan books may be purchased for educational, business or sales promotional use. For information, please email the Sales Department at sales@13thandjoan.com.

Printed in the U. S. A.

First Printing, February 2022.

Library of Congress Cataloging-in-Publication Data has been applied for.

ISBN: 978-1-953156-37-2

This book is dedicated to New York women who continue to DREAM in spite of what surrounds you.

God, I thank you for being my everything and for allowing all of the necessary to happen whether it was good or bad. They were the building blocks for me to become who I am today.

To my son K.J., thank you for being my heartbeat in tangible form. Your belief in me even when I couldn't believe in myself inspired me so much.

To my dearest family and friends and supporters, thank you for understanding who I am and loving me endlessly. Your loyalty is an endless song in my ears.

"I do not want to be idolized; I want to be an inspiration!"

Maralyn Budd

Contents

My Mother 7

Livin' Sweet on St. Mary's Street 9

Fatherless Child 13

My Healing Through Your Feeling 17

G-Code 21

The Brown Ballerina 25

No Question 29

My Perfect Guy Prayer 33

The Heart of a Project Chick 37

A True Mustang 41

Mama Mete 45

Dancing Beyond the Veil 49

Hi...I'm Insecurity 53

Time 57

Abandoned 61

The Keys to My Own Damnation 65

Single Young Mother Blues—Everyday Superheroes 69

I'm the LIFE of the Party 73

He/She 77

Silent Goodbye 81

KITTY 85

Mimi Jessica Parker	89
Play It Back	93
Just Friends	97
Ice	101
Harlem's Favorite Lady	103
Interrogation	105
I Waited	109
His Blood	113
Heaven	117
Dolly Bumblebee	121
Church Hurt	125
Shelter Who?	129
1118	135
St. Mary's Angel in Disguise	137
Had to Let You Go	141
Blood Clot NOT	145
I Am Your Reflection	149
Abba	153
The Legacy Through Me	157
I Forgive Me	163
Epilogue	166

Foreword by
Maureen Carter

As I enter a new phase in my life, I marvel at how young women are claiming their destiny. As a Black woman, I know the struggles and I know the wins. It's not all a challenge, but it's all about what you make of it. Transitions will come in life for us all, and what matters is how we deal with them. I am beginning to see that the evolution of the Black Woman is a constant sport. We must train for it, foster it, and maintain it. I am blessed to be a part of this young woman's journey. When I see another sister full of zest and zeal, I cannot help but to be onboard.

Maralyn has been sharing this book concept with me for a few years now. As her mentor and friend, I believe in her purpose and her cause. I ponder on our similarities as she is a single mom raising a talented son and on that level I cannot relate. However, I am a teenage mom who was forced to give her child up at birth to have a better life for the both of us. For that I am grateful! My daughter is a married woman now and I reconnected with her 10 years ago and she will always be my best friend! I remain strong and steadfast. God is good and He continues to give us guidance in our lives to make the journey what He wants us to have.

When I was asked to write this Foreword, I was a bit surprised because I had never written a Foreword before and I wanted to ensure that I did justice to Maralyn's authorial debut. However, Maralyn warms my heart each and every time we connect, so there was no question, I had to do it. Maralyn is a free spirit with a lot to offer the world! Supporting her on this quest is an honor and I hope and pray that everyone that reads her words will resonate with a new mantra I am sending to you - . "I am good enough! I am worth it!"

Thank you Maralyn for sharing your story, as it will touch and move others for generations to come.

Salute and blessings!!
Maureen Carter
Vice President
Design & UX at BET Networks (A subsidiary of Viacom Networks)

Introduction

New York, New York, the city that NEVER sleeps! They say if you can make it here, you can make it anywhere! When you hear the name "New York," an unexpected rush of imagination, inspiration, and so many other feelings automatically circulate through your veins and excitement consumes your soul.

From being mesmerized by the bright lights to having anxiety from the non-stop traffic, your ears are filled by the voices of cars honking as you observe New Yorkers flipping the bird at each other. You can smell the smoke from the food stands as you choke on the smoke from construction sites. The hustlers flip and dance to the music blasting, hoping someone will notice and they will finally get their big break. There are homeless people on and off the streets and trains as they continue to beg for a dollar to get a quick meal or a swipe from your MetroCard to sleep somewhere warm along the subway. You get it all!

As for me, living in the Big Apple wasn't all it appeared to be. There were times I had a season of fairy tales and there were times I damn near drowned from being choked by the pressures of having to be strong and courageous to survive in such a jungle. There are real-life lions, tigers, and bears out there waiting for you to slip and fall, leaving you no choice but to fight to survive.

There are more layers than you can imagine within this "concrete jungle." There's another world within where the drug dealers play with the lives of the druggies who stay. The fecal matter that creates a mosaic of art on project elevator walls as the urine creates a stench in the staircases that is permanent in one's soul. Shootouts are our symphony and our version of being in full frontal fashion is wearing a bulletproof vest, blades, guns, and even pepper spray. Some of us get creative and make homemade weapons. There is a struggle within the cracks of the glam of New York that society is afraid to unveil. Those people who live in hopeless dreams are the same ones who use what they have to rise from the dust and create success from ashes. I was one of those people.

Growing up in poverty yet having BIG dreams was all a poor Afro-Latina girl from the Bronx ever imagined. You have so many obstacles in front of you and the pressures of life don't allow you to dream nor give you an opportunity to imagine that your dreams can be bigger than your environment. I've experienced so much in my life thus far and I chose to be brave and share it with you. God blessed me with so many tools, and with the help from the streets, I was able to sharpen them subconsciously. From working since the age of 11 packing bags and braiding hair for $6.00, to now opening my own independent production company, it took blood, sweat, and tears to overcome it all.

My overall goal for writing this poetic memoir was to be the voice for the voiceless people like me that are afraid to speak on real life issues that society prohibits us to discuss. We as women of minority, especially from a city such as New York, have been taught to conceal our wounds and put on this persona of strength. To always be strong and never show weakness, therefore creating a strong exterior. We are walking glass houses. We were never given the chance to be transparent about the many things we deal with behind closed doors. We are told to show perfection, beauty, and peace; meanwhile, we are broken and yearning for a helping hand on the inside. I want to be able to show other women, and even men, that they are not alone. I understand because I have experienced it as well, and you do not have to be afraid to speak your truth. Deal with those skeletons and demons you battle with daily so you can be bold and be a vessel for someone waiting to be saved.

This book is dedicated to New York. It is what made me who I am today. I wouldn't have survived if I didn't learn the life lessons New York had to show me. It was my parent when I felt I had none. It was my comforter when I needed an outlet of safety. It was everything I needed it to be. I pray this first phase of my life will be a blessing to you and inspire you to live your truth, accept your truth, and push forward in spite of what your truth reveals. God is everywhere but people don't know because they have never been taught to see. It is up to us to reveal who God really is and what He has done for us through our pain and victories. You have to know that if it wasn't for God, I would honestly be dead by my own hand. God saved me. He can and will save you too. My story is just the beginning. It is merely a seed that needs to be planted in you to grow to show you that God has been and will always be with you.

With all of my Love,
M

My Mother

This is the first poem I ever wrote in my life. I was only nine years old and was going to a community center in the Bronx within the projects I was raised in called The Boston Secor Houses. While going to the afterschool program, I joined a writing program led by a woman named Colleen E. Booth. She was a published author and a performing artist. She helped give birth to my interest in writing and acting, which became a true love of mine as time passed. She taught me how to express myself, which was so hard to do because I felt so misunderstood and alone. My mom was a single parent of six, a substance abuse user, and a domestic violence survivor. We moved to this housing project through a safety transfer to get away from my father, who abused my mother and was a substance abuse user himself. I didn't really understand all that was going on at that age, so at that time my mom was someone I looked up to and adored so much. I had no idea where the love of these two avenues within the performing arts would take me.

My Mother, My Mother,
She is so so sweet,
When she puts on my shoes it tickles my feet.

My Mother, My Mother,
She brings me out to play,
I am so tired it's been a wonderful day.

My Mother, My Mother,
She is so, so fine,
Let me go to sleep and relax my mind.☺

Livin' Sweet on St. Mary's Street

Prior to moving uptown to the projects, I grew up in the streets of the South Bronx. During the '80s and '90s, drugs were at an all-time high, crack houses were a place to play in, our form of a beautiful view was the broken rubble from buildings turned to decay, and drug users that escaped from Lincoln Hospital dying on park benches from overdoses was a typical sight to see. I mean you name it! I had seen so much as a child and it really impacted major parts of my life, yet inspired me to want more for myself. In spite of living in poverty and struggling to survive, in spite of what was going on around us, we created so many memories that I cherish forever, and some that taunt me till this day. It was a safe haven for some of us that had nothing. We literally were all that we had, and we used that to live. It was so genuine and light. We didn't have much, but what we had was enough. We had each other, the entire neighborhood, all one, brothers and sisters, second mothers and fathers, aunts, uncles, and even down to the grandparents. And that was worth more than anything money could ever buy. St Mary's saved a lot of us that knew there was no way out.

St. Mary
She was our protector
Our intangible provider
Priceless in her transparency
She was our lovely day
Awakened, I arise to her kiss
A ray of light on my eyes
I embark on a new day

Summer's heat gently clams our flesh,
Sweet scent of summertime revives the hopeless

Our laughter as the fire hydrants regurgitate
Water that beats onto my skin
The poor to live in the moment
Beatboxers building bridges
To the hip-hop we hear today

Thick gold chains and leather vests
Pimps and playas sit pretty on stoops with diamond girls,
Making love to Mary Jane
Drugs smothered the streets
The lost drift into eternity
Riding park benches, where they laid, they stayed

Mama playing Bill Withers with the window wide open
Basking in the aroma of hickory
Happiness is a familiar tune
Vanilla, Chocolate, and Strawberry
These were the days a girl looked forward to

Breakers battle on beads of sweat stained cement
Gathering as one happy family
Parents watch routines created in the hallways
Dancing for hours to endless love stories
St. Mary
She was our peace
Omnipresent
Priceless in her transparency
She was our lovely day

Fatherless Child

My father was a quiet storm. He was so gentle with us, but when he was using, he became a hurricane with my mom. My father had a love for music, which was passed down to my brothers. He was the life of the party in spite of his flaws. I get my humor from him. My mom had to remain a stay-home wife because she couldn't even hold a job with how possessive, abusive, and aggressive he was with her. She tried to stay with him not only because of love, but because of us. When my parents divorced, he divorced us, his children. He was never in my life the way a father should have been. His absence impacted my life as a young girl growing into her womanhood yearning for that fatherly love. Due to his mind being so clouded with drugs and the street life, he was unable to teach and show me the intimacy and love from a father to daughter, thus resulting in issues as I dealt with men due to not knowing what I should have, my worth, and how I should be treated.

There once was a girl
Yearning for his embrace
Rescuing her from wolves
As they slowly devour her innocence
Wanting the experience of embarrassment
From friends to her first love
Wanting to call him when she was brokenhearted
Wanting that presence as she prepared for Prom
Tears of joy as he consoles her during her graduation
Dancing under the moonlight on her wedding night
Encouraging her as she lay in the hospital bed
Sacrificing her life for another
Furthering his legacy into the world.

There once was a girl
Searching for his authoritative love
Keeping her in line as she thought of sneaking out at night

Embedding fear in her
To stay away from bad boys
That "One of a Kind" kind of love
No man could ever invest in her entire being
Emulating the kind of man she would dream and aspire to have
The perfect father she dreamed of going on dates with
Mirrors how a man is supposed to treat her
How he is to love her
How she is to love him back.

There once was a girl
Who lacked all of that
These dreams mere figments of her imagination
Reality contaminates and creates love in a hopeless place
The product of a fatherless child
Seeing her perfect father intoxicated
Drugs invade her safe haven
Using his hands to express love to her mother violently
Using powder to ruin her dress
She prepares to go out with family
Crazy glue the keyhole to keep us out
We go to a shelter
Doing her best to shelter us from the abuse
Threw us away like meat to lions
Showed no embrace
Showed no guilt
Executed no protection

This girl was alone
In a world full of sharks
No knowledge of how to love someone
Or how a man is supposed to love her
Unable to permit a man to lead his family
She was placed on a silver platter perfectly imperfect
The vultures eager to devour her soul
Tigers toss her back and forth like a plush doll
Bears eat the sweet honey left in her soul
She is a fatherless child

Hopeless
Only the scars of memory from the abuse
Lacking love and intimacy, father to daughter
Alone
A figment to her very own dreams

My Healing Through Your Feeling

I was molested at a young age by a very close family member. It affected me in ways I would have never imagined, more than I realized throughout my life. From the lack of trust I constantly displayed to those closest to me, to developing and having chronic insecurities which festered into every part of my life, especially relationships. Being a victim of this kind of abuse, you subconsciously develop psychological and other mental health issues. I never dealt with that level of trauma and I didn't know how to. So when I had my son, I was so overprotective of him because I feared someone could take his innocence away as mine was taken away. A lot of women of minority groups have gone through this, and it seemed so taboo and forbidden to speak about during my upbringing. Society overlooks it and fails to see it is a silent hurricane destroying so many women behind closed doors. It was always swept under the rug. Families who have done so have no idea the mental instability that can stem from not dealing with it; the trust issues and the insecurities that are created and fester if we don't deal with and talk about it in real time.

Lights out
Sound asleep
You come into my territory
Invade my comfort zone
Rob me of my dreams
With a contaminated kiss
An inappropriate touch
Body to body
Forced with no consent
Silently destroying my tomorrow

So young
So innocent
So blind
So naïve
You win, I lose
Gaining insecurities
Deceit
Lack of trust and sorrow
Seeds you planted
Lay bloom to torment me of my purest thoughts
I can't shake it
Taking over, no invitation
I can't look at you
Feelings of anguish and disgust
As the crickets whisper and the streetlights dance alone
Left there to ponder my own guilt
Did I allow this to happen?
How could I have prevented it?
Drowning in my own blood
No life boat
No SOS
Trying to understand
Why family would do such a thing
Who can I run to when brokenhearted?
Who would defend me?
Defending myself from every man,
Willing to drown trying to rescue me
They drown because I refuse to be saved
I fail yet again
I run from man to man
Try every way to ruin them so they can't ruin me
In search of what's missing
You more than robbed me
Stealing dreams of forever wanting to hold someone,
A limitless love
Time after time
Relationship after relationship
The love I try to give but can't
Afraid they will invade my territory,

Pillaging what's left of me.
A woman scorned by her own blood
I lay there
My heart convicts me to let them go
How unfair it is for them
Trying to mend broken pieces,
This void that you created
Constant thoughts of dirt you embedded under my skin
A permanent stench
I can't scrub it off.

One day at a time
One smile every hour
One "I forgive you" as the days dance into the sunset
One prayer to HIM, now endless conversations
I slowly peeled the shame off of my soul
I confidently smiled and learned to love every inch of me
Even the parts that were violated
Even the parts that include you
I forgive you

G-Code

To Henrietta

My maternal grandmother was the end product of a love triangle between an African American man, who was my great-grandfather, and a German married woman, who was my great grandmother. She was given up for adoption to an orphanage, due to her being "a nigger baby," during The Great Depression era when Jim Crow laws and segregation, which stemmed from racism, were at an all-time high. My grandmother endured so much during her time in the foster care system in which I personally believe caused drinking to be her outlet when she became an adult, due to it helping her suppress all the pain and suffering she endured throughout her life. She had other brothers and sisters who she was reunited with years ago, as they were searching for her as well. Though there was one who didn't want to be bothered because she was Black. He ended up dropping dead in a supermarket. In spite of all my grandmother endured, she is one of the most influential women I have come to know and a hero who conquered so much and was so strong. She is one of the most boisterous, humorous, dancing machines, freestyle rapping, "I'm a movement by myself," amazing, and captivating women I know. Everyone loves Ms. Henny.

Born an orphan
To a White woman caught in a love triangle
Shipped away cause the "nigger" in her may show
As the days bloom and she begins to grow
Carries an intoxicated elegance
Captivating those exposed to her presence
Full length mink and red nail polish
Her walk exudes authority
Slurred speech put smiles on those she encountered,
Miss Henny to the naysayers
My everything
"Cherrycone"
Pop locking and twerking,
The original dance machine.
From the strippers to old dippers.
Singing Etta James as she grabs me to dance
We laugh.
She's the highlight of every function
Best friends with every host on 107.5 WBLS and 98.7 KISS FM,
She sways to the symphonic tunes
Serenades with *Majorska* and *Pall Malls*
She creates her own stage.
As she naps on the couch hallucinating of "gigantuah"
Waking her up from her tormenting dreams
The troubles inflicted in foster care
She was bold, conquering them with her spunk.
Courageous
Rap battles off beat,
Don't get hit with that right hook
Humor lighting up the darkest room
I stare in admiration of her
Looking past her flaws,
My "G-Code"

The Brown Ballerina

Up until I became a mom at 19 years-old, I was a dancer for as long as I could remember. Throughout my time as a serious dancer I was exposed to what really happens in that arena, especially during the times when minority dancers were not popular and were seen as foreign. There were no "Black Ballerina" movements like there are today, nor any social media outlets to really push your talent, so the process was so much harder. I was my own voice. I worked hard enough to obtain a scholarship at The Dance Theatre of Harlem. The pressure to want to make it was so high at such a young age, you would do whatever you could. In my case, because my build is more muscular, I was told by a high-level administrator in a prestigious company to eat less carbohydrates. I didn't even understand what a carbohydrate was! Plus dealing with colorism, racism, and never being good enough... it took a toll on me. With no one to help me and guide me, I looked to a friend for advice. Shortly after that, I developed eating disorders - anorexia and bulimia. I was absolutely blind to what I was doing to my body. I just wanted to make it out of the projects and buy my family a house and not suffer anymore. I did what I needed but it only resulted in sickness. Until this day I suffer from gastrointestinal issues from something that happened 20 years ago. I really didn't have an advocate to push me and guide me. My mother was a single parent and worked three jobs and I traveled alone back and forth to dance classes. My son is a scholarship student at Alvin Ailey American Dance Theatre. I speak life into him every day and let him know that he is perfect the way God made him. For me, I wish there was a voice to have saved me from my own demise. I could have been so much further.

Entering a room full of snowflakes
Dressed to perfection
Perfect buns, pretty pink shoes
Leotards clean and pressed
Thin, frail, graceful skeletons anxiously await

Mothers fixing gowns while Fathers talk on phones
In awe at their perfection, or so you think

Here you stand, the brown ballerina
Your muscular body not built for grace
Mommy's working three jobs
Father more than a phone call away
Still you exude gentle authority
That power that intimidates them
They silently cast you out
You don't fit
Eat less and dance more
They tell you
The pressure suffocates you
You run back to that place of peace
Where dreams danced with your imagination
Wanting to make your mark known as the brown ballerina
It's okay Black girl, you will get a solo one day
It's okay Black girl, you will eventually be a principal
You encourage yourself
You're all you have
So, you work,
Hard. Night after night
Dancing in your small room
Janet Jackson is your melody
You stretch
200 crunches a night
You eat less
No carbs, no carbs, just dance
Blisters house themselves on your feet
You can barely walk
The pain grips you
So you ice your entire being
You see the imprint of your skeleton
Though it's not good enough
So you continue to push

4, 5, to 6 days a week
No life
No friends
Class after class
As sweat cascades down the lining of your spine
you push to do an arabesque
As lightheaded as you may feel
Maintain your alignment
GRAND JETE'
You nail it
They nod, yet praise the others while you sweat the most
It's double work for you
What are the odds?
You have nothing to lose so you give it your all
Borrowing money from family members
Mommy can't afford dance school
Single mother, six kids, three jobs
Born and raised in the South Bronx
Elevators were a work of art
Painted with urine and fecal matter
Praying that you will one day save them from this torment
It's all up to you
So, you work to invest in your dream

After the sweat evaporates
After the blisters begin to heal
After the muscle aches subside
You then realize
I will never be that Black ballerina in swan lake
They only tolerate me
I am a ghost in their kingdom
I will never be the hero for my family
I am yet another slave
Doing pirouettes near their crisp waters
They just allow me to play dress up

No Question

I was introduced to hip-hop dancing as a child and my life was never the same. During my upbringing in the projects, I met a group of girls that impacted my life. They don't even know it but they taught me the meaning of sisterhood. I went through a battle of dancing hip-hop and not being ashamed of my body to going to classical ballet class and thinking everything was wrong with me. We had nothing yet we had everything. We used what we had and created a movement not just for us but for communities. It was so much bigger than us. We traveled all over together competing with other dance companies to be performers at the legendary Apollo Theater. Growing up in the projects and being a local legend to voiceless souls, I remember every year people from all five boroughs would come to our projects in August for our annual block party to watch us perform. I never understood the impact as a child but now as an adult I see. They waited hours in anticipation to watch us perform. I have learned that people are always watching, and you always have to put your best foot forward for our purposes in life are not about us, it is really bigger than you.

Founded in the bathroom at Hostos
We tightened our ponytails and fixed our skirts
Walking towards a crowd that anticipated a great time
Three of us
With nothing to lose and the respect of representing to gain
We confidently walked on stage
Gave it our all
Winning was only the beginning

Eight ladies
Jalene, Deeshow, Nisha, Thithi, Phyllis, Vanessa, Ashley, and myself
A sisterhood no one could ever break
From fist fights to countless draining rehearsals
Learning from hip-hop legends

Building in a broken society
Ms. Diane sewed outfits and managed us
Faye's gift of gab got us hookups
Ms. Adane, the warden
Ms. Lucy's rice and beans, trips to McDonald's on Tuesdays
I carry a
plastic bag filled with $5.00 worth of pennies
From multicolored wigs to cowgirl hats
Hopes to make it to unknown heights
We were the role models of hopeless souls
Saturated in their very own deferred dreams
We looked out for each other; inseparable
A movement
The main event at block parties
Winning The All Stars competition
becoming the faces of a clothing line
Victorious at the Apollo
Conquering the dreams, we conjured as a unit
To be bigger than the environment we grew up in
Without a question, we were the answer to many
Reppin' for our block as they traveled in packs to come support us
They were for us.

But time began to deteriorate
Pregnancy evaded some
Others just got tired and wanted more
We split and carried on creating new paths in life
We faced the authenticity of our realities
Made choices based on our needs
Many waited on our comeback, but it faded away
A dream deterred
The silver lining the clouds that reside above the Bronx,
Now tarnished.

No matter how far any of us may be,
What we may have ended up becoming
We were, and still are, the inspiration to many
The mountains we moved out of the very lives of the hopeless

Allowing the sky to crack open and the sun shined in on their despair
We gave them hope
Engulfed on what others would never dare to see, let alone try
Our name will forever ring bells
Cause this is how we got down with No Question

My Perfect Guy Prayer

When I was a little girl, after seeing what my mother endured with my father and other men, I said a prayer to God regarding "the guy of my dreams" that I desired when I became a woman, and all the qualities I wanted in my soon-to-be-one-day husband. I vowed to never encounter a love like the kind my mother experienced. I prayed and prayed to Abba for "The One." Now I have experienced some wins and losses from guys. However, I still believe he is out there, and is being prepared for me as I am being prepared for him.

As my pen touches the paper
As my tears soar down my pores
My sorrows sleep with the "I'm sorry" he left at my doorstep
Side by side with the decaying roses

I sit silently and talk to Abba
Praying that one day, my smiles will be eternal
My heart will dance into forevermore conjoined with "the one"
I reflect
Travel back in time
To witness the toxic love my mother endured
Intense festering beyond borders
Love trapped in a deserted paradise
Making a forever promise to my soul that one day
God's divine love would reflect from his creation's being into my soul
Two different energies, yet one purpose
So, I write
Pen to paper
Heart to prayer

His heart, to dwell in the oceans of God's promises
Forever lost and honored there

I am never afraid to pray with and for him
He prays for me more than I pray for myself,
Honoring his alone time with God
Seeking to be a better man as the days fade away
Taller than me, he suffocates me in his arms
There I will sleep
Swag speaking for itself
Trendsetter with his style
Finds ways to change the game
He is smart, funny, and empathetic
Stands his ground
No bullshit
He is gentle yet so strong
Overpowers the fight I display before every man who combats me
I fall into his territory, willingly
My submission is pure
His words of wisdom paint themselves on the sleeves of my soul.
He knows what he wants
He goes for it even through the obstacles
His desire is to impact the world with his being
One song at a time, one speech closer
He loves and takes pride in his family
Understands the importance of sustaining it
He worships my body, loving every inch of it
Even the stretch marks that were created to bring forth our legacy
Only seeing me, the only woman in the world
In a room full of vultures, waiting to devour him with lust and lies
He only sees me as I see him
Eager to come home and caress every inch of it
Stroking his fingers through my hair
With every kiss, every embrace
I feel most secure with him
As he does with me
Laughing as we make love
Crying when we are weary
Transparency is our tool to longevity
Communication is our battle plan
He challenges me to do better

To be better by creating a better self
Hand on the arch of my back as he pushes me,
Conquering the very demons contaminating the world
As I do the same for him.
We stand together, never letting go
Taking one step at a time to heal
as much of the world as we can through the love confined in our hearts
Conversations are beyond what the earth can fathom
His smile captivates souls and sets free the bound
His walk, his talk, his endless sarcasm
I met my match
He emulates the true meaning of a real man
Young Black men sit and grab jewels from him
He is a teacher, preaching how to survive as the world doesn't care
Teaches our son how to put on a tie
I stand at the door in amazement
Takes our daughter on dates
Showering her with the world and showing her how a man is supposed to treat her
I look out the window as he opens the car door for her to enter
I smile
He is the key to my heart
The very thought of him overwhelms my soul
I am alive and grateful to wake up beside him every day
Hearts beat as one, conjoined
The only man that dwells the same place God and my children do
He is my perfect guy

The Heart of a Project Chick

I grew up in areas that people are afraid to drive by, let alone walk through. The stereotypes and perceptions of people who live in these areas however are so disheartening. We, especially as women, who live in the "ghetto" areas, or as the correct term is, "impoverished," never really get a chance to show the world who we really are. People don't know about what we endure, our strengths, and what we possess within that society doesn't see. There is this perception that we are so hard, angry, strong, and bitter, when really, we are gentle creatures that are fragile, waiting for someone to love us and create the opportunity for us to show how great and magical we really are. I dedicate this poem to the people, especially the women, who live in the real concrete jungles of New York.

Bamboo earrings, long press-on nails, and a loud mouth
That's what society has taught them to see in me
The ignorant one,
A limited vocabulary in the wrong context,
Flamboyant personality and dramatic gestures cry out "a woman scorned."
Playing the tough, strong minority role as if the world owes her something
The angry Black woman who has a bitter soul
The loud Hispanic that speaks way too fast,
Exuding sex from the crown of her head to the very soles of her feet
The same ghetto "hoodrat" that brings her tribe of kids,
Cursing and yelling at them like dogs on the street
"Oh yeah, her!"
She never had dreams and goals
Too busy being fast; the high school dropout
Her dreams can't ever be astronomical
Project chicks only collect food stamps and live off of welfare, right?

We don't have feelings because we are so tough yet dumb
We are not worthy enough to become the wife to any man
Only a mother to numerous sons.

You have no idea what resides in the heart of a "project chick."
That woman you see and think is so thorough is really afraid
She uses her voice to stay alive
That's all she has left,
Pushing beyond measure.
She is a fighter in every way possible.
She sacrifices herself for what she only knows
Works three jobs so she can take care of the children
Conceived with he, the man she thought would be her endless love
The very same man that left after abusing her for years in her child's eyes.
The same man who tried to rape her daughter and used drugs in their sight
She once dreamed of a house with the picket fence
She found love after love when all along she was only looking for someone
To fill the voids that blossomed into holes in her soul
Or what about the girl cursing nonstop and hasn't even reached 18
She acts out as an outlet to conceal the pain,
Being raped at 11,
Thrown away in exchange for drugs

Those who were "brothers" embrace each other one minute,
then next become participants in a gory fist fight
Deadly shootouts in the crisp summer air
These were our fireworks in the Bronx
Money Takers and Dead Soldiers,
Raised by parent gangs that teach them
To bully innocent people and fight till the death

Fecal matter and urine create a torturing aroma in the staircases and elevators
The elderly pass out on 10 flight walk-ups as a consequence of broken elevators
The crack houses and the crackheads that dwell in them
Dealers hanging in hallways day and night,
Killing their own kind for chump change

Your soul has no choice but to embrace it or allow it to slowly kill you
Where else can you run to?
Where else can you go?
Who will lend a helping hand,
Genuinely without wanting a sexual favor in return?
So, you stay, and work on yourself the best way you know how
Getting in position until you see a door of escape and burst through it

What about the woman that cries at night because she doesn't know how to change?
What about the woman that was never taught how to love someone,
Using the only thing she has to survive?
She doesn't know how to love
Because love has only been a four-letter word to her
Used only to gain access to her most precious rubies that have worth
So she lies in her own contamination and dies slowly
Losing herself, yet finding the only way she will escape

Please know that not every "project chick" is on welfare or has five kids
Not every "project chick" gives it up easy
Not every "project chick" speaks Ebonics and has poor manners
There are "project chicks" who have degrees beyond degrees
"Project chicks" who have become millionaires and started successful businesses
And "project chicks" who have changed the very same communities they grew up in.
Just know not every "project chick" is what you perceive them to be
We carry our strength and become the conquerors of tomorrow
We demolish the generational curses that stand today
Because the heart of a "project chick" doesn't fit into your perception
We defeat the biggest battle; the contaminated identity society has labeled us to as
We are human just like you

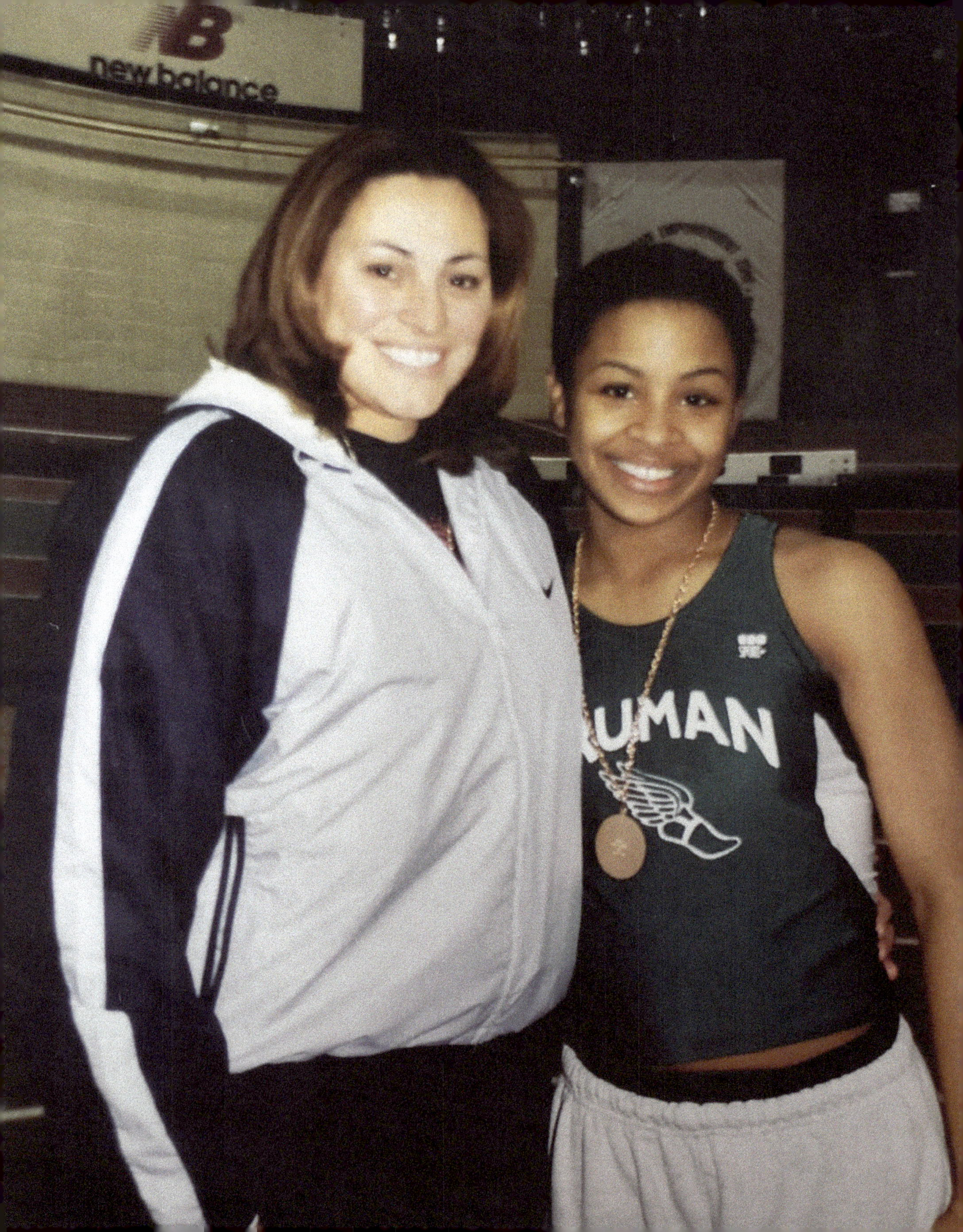
new balance
UMAN

A True Mustang

*To Miss

To be honest, my teenage/high school years were the worst yet best years of my upbringing. I was on the varsity track team and ran throughout high school. It literally saved my life. I was introduced to a woman by the name of Maritza Osorio aka "Miss." She saved me by encouraging me to try out for the track team the same day I was going to get initiated into a gang. I remember the day of tryouts. I was so conflicted all day in school; and then in 8th period, while walking down the stairs, I made the decision to not get initiated into the gang, and my life has never been the same. It was either stay on the streets or run track, so I chose to run track. I experienced so much. I got to travel and was introduced to a different kind of sisterhood that I cherish to this very day. During those years I did endure peer pressure, suicide, anger, homosexuality, depression, low self-esteem, puberty, sex, and bullying. Though I experienced all of that, I wouldn't trade it for anything. Thank you Miss, for saving me from myself.

Starting block into an unknown territory
Because of you, I chose the unknown over my bond with the streets
Saving me from a life of gangbanging with those that would later on deceive me
A life of being locked up, shot up, or dead
God had grace over me
He assigned me to you
My life had changed
Remodeling a bad attitude and a treasure chest full of hurt
You looked past all of that and embraced me
Providing a special kind of love unforeseen to me
Pushing me to limits unknown
Sprints, hurdles, stairs, lunges

Transforming me into who I was to become
Waking up at 5 a.m. for the Hispanic games and
Meets at Colgate sponsored races.
So angry at the discipline I needed to learn
Losing what I was familiar with to only gain so much more
I gained a lifetime of friendships
I gained an endless love with loyalty
I gained my high school diploma
I gained a brighter future
Understanding the meaning of what it meant to be a true "Mustang."
Not just on the track but to gallop into life with courage
No matter what cards you were dealt
I gained a mother that would slap me in front of the school without a care
Who dealt with the person I was and claimed me anyway.
You were never ashamed of your girls
Even when it seemed as if the world was against me
Dancing for a talent show and parts of my being wanted the shine
Videos galore captured on the memories of loved ones' camcorders
My breast will forever have a name
But my character was brought to shame
For an incident that wasn't my fault, yet I got the blame
Suspension and banned from running for two track meets
You stood there and claimed me as yours and never let go
When my teammates and I secretly took silly boob pics in the night at the
Walt Disney Relays
Running nude as a dare at Penn Relays
Flipping tables in anger at track meets
Secret lovers with each other
Fist fights in the locker room
In spite of all that, you stayed with us and protected us
Strong yet so gentle, and loved us no matter what
Picking up the pieces of our mistakes yet still holding our hands with a smile
You saved me from the lions, tigers, and bears
Laughs in your house and cries on the track
I ran towards a brighter future because of you
You saved me from myself
You showed me another door I never knew was there
I thank God for your endless love that still carries on today

Your discipline helped mold me into the woman I am today
You were my heaven-sent mother in disguise
Thank You, Miss

Mama Mete

I met Deborah Mete in 2001 at an indoor track game. We met as her son and I were on the same track team and very close; and as the saying goes, the rest was history. She has been my spiritual mom, guiding and supporting me throughout my life during the most trying times. She was always by my side even when I ran away. I consider her the mother I never had, the mother I always wanted. She was one of the women who filled the voids in my life that my mom was unable to fill.

They say you only get one Mother
I believe God had other plans
Meeting through your flesh, I became your blood
As you held the embarrassing signs consumed with glitter
Cheering us on to win the race, your encouragement struck a nerve
I knew from that day on, my life would never be the same
You were God's gift to me when hopelessness evaded my thoughts
Constantly praying for me and pulling me to safety even when I pushed you away
Your dramatic antics was a reflection of who I was,
So our bond was inseparable
You love me as if I am your own
The warden, as we say,
As strict as you may have been,
your love conquered all.
When I couldn't hear my own thoughts,
You would call and calm the winds that made me
Choke on my own dismay with words of encouragement
Your wisdom resides within the depths of my soul
Your surprise visits would light up my entire being
Even when I knew the price I had to pay
Dinner dates and shopping till our knees burned off

It was always worth it
Your loyalty defeated the very demons of trust that I couldn't combat
You knew my heart and you kept it safe
I was a reflection of your life story
In your own unique way you protected it as much as you could
As they didn't understand what we had, we didn't care and kept loving in spite of
You pushed me back into the arms of Abba
I was able to trust Him again,
Your dedication redefining my perception
Without limitation
Refusing condemnation
You gave me inspiration
A 9/11 survivor willing to give your life for those who choked on their own blood
You were and still are a warrior
My warrior
Over 16 years of endless love
You give me a reason to go on, to press even when I don't feel the release button
You are more than just a spiritual mother
You are my Angel and I wouldn't trade you for the world
My sweet Mama Mete

Dancing Beyond the Veil

*To Enetha

I was introduced to liturgical dancing at the age of 13 by a woman named Enetha Kelly. I remember going into the church with my brother's ex-girlfriend and at the end of the sermon they called up people who had never been there before and asked them why they wanted to join the church. The sermon that day spoke on holding your own sword to fight against the enemy, so I told them just that! "I want to be able to hold my own sword." I was already dealing with depression and suicidal thoughts, which I kept to myself, and I thought maybe they could really help me. I made the decision to join a Pentecostal church home after not being in the Catholic church for years since my parents divorce. I learned so much, both good and bad. Being a professional dancer and having professional dance training, it was definitely a different style of dance that allowed me to connect to God on a level I never knew I could. I learned what intimacy through dance was like. Actually being free and allowing your spirit to dance through you. People have this perception that praise dancing is nothing but Black women just dancing and being emotional, but it is so much more than that. This type of dancing has brought healing to the sick and deliverance to the bound. It was a newfound love for me.

I gazed in awe, watching her
I was 13
Gracefully lifting her hands,
Taking a deep breath
With every move
Her dance is her weapon
So intimate
So graceful
She is at peace with herself
A moment in time
Frozen between Creator and creation

Lasting only a few minutes
My heart opens up
To a new kind of dance
A new kind of worship
Only Abba Himself understands
Spontaneous before Him
I pour my hidden emotions at His feet
The alabaster box I've carried for years
All of my sorrow
All of my joy
Given to Him where time is eternal
As the Angels dance beside me
Hand by hand
I hear the cries of His people
They were blessed and set free
I was the vessel
One of the hardest battles I have to fight
Dancing for the world vs dancing beyond the veil
Trying to reveal what they can't comprehend
Dancing through the sorrows of yesterday
Dancing through the joys of today
Dancing through the fear of tomorrow
I fast before Him
Preparing my body as a living sacrifice
Someone was healed through the dance
Someone was set free through my worship
I stretch and meditate
My brokenness is the fuel that pushes me to fight for them
It's bigger than me
Conquering the very demons that torment HIS people
That torment me
My feet move one step closer to the battlefield
My armor is on, protecting me
Bleeding till I've slain
We are one heartbeat
We conquer together
We win together
We soar into freedom with Abba behind us

We are His warriors
Pushing into another dimension
As we dance beyond the veil

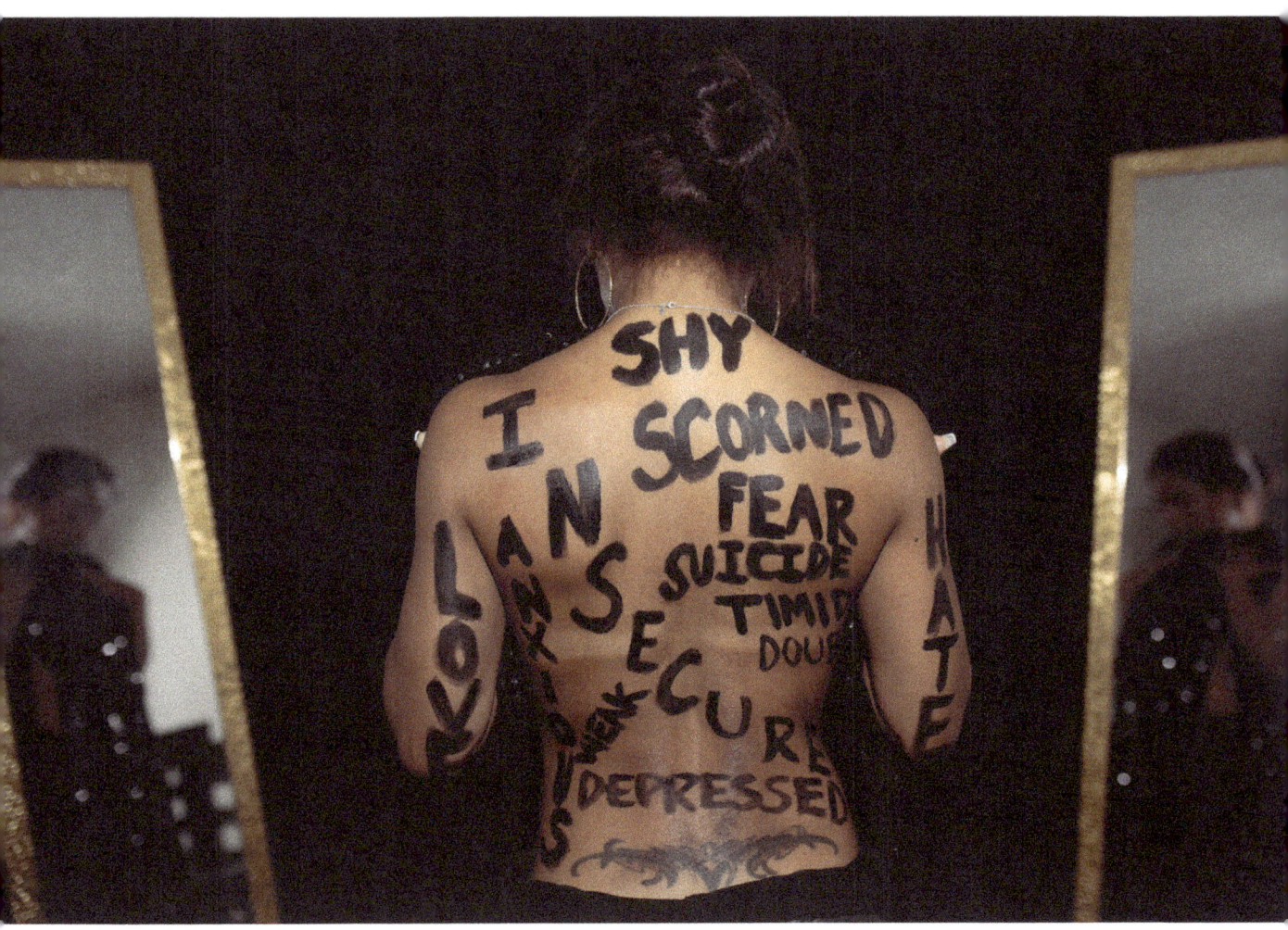

Hi...I'm Insecurity

As a woman who is told on a daily basis how beautiful I am and who is constantly complimented and offered so many things from men and women, I too deal with insecurities and thoughts of feeling inadequate. There were times that this feeling of not being "good enough" debilitated me. I became so depressed at times because of the pressures of societal standards that make you believe you will never beat this invisible level they have created that was never really there in the first place. It's amazing how people can look so polished and perfect yet be bleeding and decaying on the inside. People admired me so much and thought I was so beautiful, however, I felt so ugly and hated myself at one point in my life. We as women mask those dark, painful feelings underneath our beauty every day and are so afraid to speak to other women about it. We then go against each other and bring each other down as opposed to uplifting and building each other up. Society has created this mindset that we are to compete with one another and not uplift the next woman. So we act catty and become jealous of each other instead of helping each other with our inner demons. We are all beautiful, internally and externally. But we choose instead to conceal it and show what man-made products can do; meanwhile we are beyond toxic internally.

Thick thighs, no hips, big bottom lip
Flapjacks for cheeks and a gap between her teeth
Empty socks for breasts. What else can be next?
That's how I saw what I mean to me
She was a late bloomer they say
She can be down because she makes us laugh
Unpredictable
As I stuffed my bra and as I straightened my shaft
I realized then that I was trying to fit in
But why?
I was always born to stand the hell out

From the great days of Hyper Piper and Diamond Girl
I never wanted to be a minion

Some years drive by and puberty knocks on my door
As I listen to Christina Aguilera's *Beautiful* on repeat,
I can feel and hear my insides silently being eaten alive
Dancing with an elite ballet school
Scholarship student at its best
I have to be mindful of what I ingest
As my character is always put to the test
I slowly malnourished my soul
From the very things that keep it whole
I then slowly die
In the same place my dreams and aspirations lie
As I see tears coming from my mother's eyes
As the doctor tries to help me
All I can say is "I am fine."
When in all actuality
I am screaming "SAVE ME!"

Oh, she's a woman now!
Just look at my strut and my smile
My catwalk captivates the audience I catered to
Red lipstick and smokey eyes
Spanx fall in love with my skin as they snug my tiny hips
Cutlets fit to perfection and there is no detection
I emulate what others dreamed to be
As I gracefully sit at the bar
I smile as they gaze and think of a masterplan
As the she lions think of a way to destroy me
With bitter words and intimidation
I flip my hair and suffocate in the lust that resides
Saturated on the walls
Embedded on the dance floor
We all gaze in suspense as the night gets older
Shoulder to shoulder we are one in sin
Ignorance tranquilizes; we are all slowly dying
I am aware of it all

Hitting me like a ton of bricks
Yet I wanted to be accepted and needed
In spite of the glamour and glitz
I am slowly dying inside
I didn't love me or who I am
I hid behind what I thought created the best in me
As I look around and notice all the others
Their beauty and some brains as they indulge in conversation
All I hear is "I will never look as good as her."
She looks better than me
I ask God why I don't have that
I think of all I had to put in to dish out
I think of all that I don't have that I'm lying about
I then crumble yet crack a smile to conceal
As I sit there in my despair
As I laugh but cry inside
As I entertain yet want to curl up and hibernate
I then embrace my inner me named insecurity

Time

Breaking up with someone is never an easy thing to do. As there is a process one must go through to reach the point of healing and moving on, there are layers of this process that we as humans never take a moment to sit and let happen. We sometimes, or should I say most times, have a tendency to just hop into another relationship because we fear being alone. I personally never knew how to deal with breakups, and because I was so broken, I always acted out in other ways to deal with it. I also never took the "time" to allow time to be just what it is. I dedicate this poem to the women and the emotional process we go through during the "time" to heal after a breakup.

They say time heals all wounds....
But does it really?
Or does it simply allow you the opportunity to reflect on how to cope with the aches?
As the days pass by I wonder why? How? When? What the fuck?
Some days I smile thinking of the memories, others I'm limp.
Blood rushing through my veins, my heart beats faster with every thought of you,
Then I realize my heart is distraught because of you,
Some days I want to run over you,
I reflect on the memories and fall back in love with you,
Never would I have imagined this feeling could ever be,
Why do I let this get to me?
Having a polar personality,
Concealed by a "Boss Bitch" mentality,
You were not a part of my strategy,
And now shit is just tragedy,
The thought of you just saddens me,
My dreams I want to become reality,
But then I realize life is but a dream,

And I will continue to float upstream,
On a boat without a paddle,
Alone…with my skirt conjoined to its seam,
So, I will continue to row this boat,
To ease the pain my heart once choked,
And gently glide towards deferred dreams,
Until the grass turns money green…

Abandoned

I was 17 years old the first time I was homeless. I had just graduated high school, the first in my family, and though things seemed as if they were going great, I woke up every day wanting to die. Due to a dispute from a misunderstanding with my biological mother, I was kicked out of her home with only a garbage bag of clothes. It came at such a trying time due to the fact that I was a month away from beginning college and constantly fought with my mother due to a lack of understanding and my feeling as if she kept putting a man before her children. At this point, my relationship with my mom was severed beyond repair. I was completely misunderstood and hated myself so much that I really thought suicide was the easier way out. This was when I began to use drugs to cope with the pain. I remember this season of being homeless. I had been sleeping on people's floors, and would frequent Central Park at night with a friend, high as ever, on their park benches, and sneaking in different parts to sleep. I slept at different men's houses, and some even tried raping me, but that was the risk I had to take for shelter. I partied all night so I could ride the trains and sleep until the sun came out, you name it! I was so numb to life, death literally was an easy way out for me.

August 17, 2004
Sent to fend on her own
Not a dollar to spare
Not a pot to piss in
Just the clothes on her back and her severed heart
Police had no care
Misunderstood
Taking the longest elevator ride in her life
Riding toward damnation
Reflecting on the could have been
A great relationship from mother to daughter
She was abandoned
Hitting her like a ton of bricks

Suffocating on the thick clouds
Residing along the lifeless streets
Floating in a dark place
Deserted, a blank open space
Asking myself over and over
How did I get here?
Graduated two months ago
First in her family
Accomplishments proudly slept on her shoulders
The shining star
The light that once shined
Died during that fight
She is worthless
Now the offspring to Mama streets and Daddy hustle
Grooming her
Taught her everything
She still failed
A broken-down palace
Credit cards reached its max
Labeled the Nomad
Bright student in college
She couldn't focus
No money to eat
Concrete mattress
Dismissed from college
The poor attendance couldn't compensate
For the money she didn't have to get there
Once again abandoned
As she lay on the park benches suffocating in despair
Hopes of getting raped, murdered, or kidnapped
The expectancy to die, living for no tomorrow
But God had other plans
Despair consuming her veins
Hatred for her mother spiraled
Weeks passed by
No call to see if she was alive
Reality hit once again; she was abandoned
Using what she had to survive

Cut off all of her glory
Consumed drugs to ease the daily torment
Trying to escape the abandonment
No matter where she turned
Her damnation, patiently waiting
So, she gracefully grabbed her hand
Cascading into the unknown
Didn't matter what was to come
She didn't care anymore
Parties didn't help
Only giving a temporary high away from the sorrow;
She drank it away
Men didn't make it better
Only getting her off to live another day
Swallowed in her misery
Laying on a red carpet smothered in mice feces
Trying to make a dollar out of infected wounds
Soaked under intoxication
Crying out to God
How could He allow such suffering?
Had a lot going for herself
How could someone called mother be so jealous?
All she tried was take her out of her own sorrows
Giving the life she deserved to have from daughter to mother
She laid back on that park bench and cried, laughed, yelled, and prayed
Embraced losing herself to the world that very moment
She abandoned herself

The Keys to My Own Damnation

I have a long history with suicide. You can say we are literally day 1s, best friends. I yearned for it so much because I was so hurt and depressed and broken beyond repair, it literally was an outlet for me. It was as if when taking the steps to taking my own life, I had a rush of exhilaration. That's when I knew something was wrong. I was manic and dealt with suicide for years and struggled so badly from overdosing on pills, cutting myself, alcoholism, and putting myself in dangerous situations with the hopes of death being the outcome. I was lost and numb to life. So many young people deal with suicidal thoughts on a daily basis and feel as if they have nobody to speak to that will understand. I endured it and my son had issues with it due to being bullied for years because people thought he was gay as he is a dancer at Alvin Ailey. I was able to understand and help him through it. If you need help, please don't ever hesitate to reach out to someone. Please talk to your children and family and listen to them, for you have no idea what they go through on a daily basis and may need rescuing from, or just an ear to hear them.

Use a knife
Bottle of pills
Jump off a bridge
Crash on a hill
Into a wall
Out I will fall
Incident so big
Yet feeling so small
The liberating feeling
As the wind blows through your hair
Anxiety as the pills dissolve through your veins
Adrenaline rush as your blood becomes one

Imprinting on blade and water
Numb to the pain
Numb to tomorrow's heartache
Domino effect of the eternal pain loved ones will feel
I fly towards eternal damnation
Uncontrollable addictive sensation
Consumed and convicted with my heart's hesitation
Overwhelmed with the power of my own desperation
I just wanted to be me
Society wouldn't let me be
Freedom was all I tried to see
Choosing to make love with eternity
At least she will soar and dance with me
Struggles of life have reached breaking points
Gave birth to the thoughts so what's the point
Daily torment yet she wears a smile
She is one with her sorrow, she is now senile
Blood boiling through my veins
Mind leaps toward the insane
Living off the leftovers from my pain
My name is only what shall remain
A distant memory
Lasting but a season
Being the catalyst to my reason
Committing the ultimate crime, treason
I'd rather soak forever with my tormenting sorrows
I'll die with no worries of a better tomorrow

Single Young Mother Blues—Everyday Superheroes

I've been a single mother for as long as I can remember. Since my son was the age of two, I have raised him alone after parting ways from his father, who cheated, in addition to things just not working out. I guess when I left him, he left my son as well. People can never fully understand the struggles, trials, and tribulations we encounter as single parents. What we endure on a daily basis can make some people want to throw in the towel and give up on life. You often blame yourself for putting your child through such a trying time. I honestly blame myself every day. s From, like the saying goes, "robbing Peter to pay Paul," to the countless payment arrangements with bills to make ends meet, mandatory childcare, food, and at times not eating so your child can and going to bed hungry but your child by the grace of God has a full belly, shelter so you won't end up homeless, emergencies, and trying build your own business, it is beyond exhausting. Waking up at 4 a.m. to get yourself mentally prepared, waking your child up, dropping them off, and picking them up from school, working full time, going to school full time. Most times it weighed so heavy on me, but the legacy must go on! You have to fight because it is so much bigger than you. I just want all the single mothers, or should I say parents, out there to know that you are not alone. You are a real-life superhero, BIGGER and better than any Batman or Superman. What we deal with has no comparison to any villain. We conquer daily villains with little to no sleep! God is the source of our strength and it's because of Him we are able to win every battle thrown our way. I know it all too well and I understand. This one's for you.

You call it an accident
I call it fate,
Based on the choices you've made
Making a decision that will change your life forever
Molding your character into something you never dreamed of
Your patience is tested
Your strength rapidly grows
Being broken down to be rebuilt again
A single young mother with no idea how to be
No more parties and being ignorant
Daily lessons transform into memories
Heart racing with internal panic
Smiling through the fear
You suck it up
Beginning to teach what you have been taught
Working and going to school full time
Mid semester breaks from lack of childcare
Sacrificing your dreams to bring forth the dreams of your heartbeat
It's worth it
Struggles come and go
Money eaten by locusts
You try to make a dollar out of nothing
Days you're so tired and don't know how you can move on
As the walls cave in and your soul gasps for air
Looking for a sign of rescue pulling all the strength you have left
Your heartbeat looks into your eyes,
Holding your face and smiles
The waves suddenly begin to calm
The wind gusts die
You can breathe again
Even when you're on the rocks,
Alone.
Barefoot in front of the endless ocean
Using your superpowers to see what's in store for tomorrow
Fear in your eyes ain't no surprise because you live in the struggle
Your heartbeat sees you and runs to their hero,
The single Mother,
The one they admire

Stand tall like the superwoman you are,
Continue to save the ones you would die for
Blood, sweat, and tears you may shed
But the look on their faces as you tuck them into bed,
So innocent and naïve to all you endure
Thinking you are saving them when they are your cure
They are the fuel to your endurance
No matter how the world labels you
Conquering the statistics by leaps and bounds
Even when the father was no longer around
You persevered
You conquered
You soared
You are the true superhero in spite of all the villains that came to combat you
You have and still are fighting the good fight
Your mistakes have not disqualified who you will become
Pat yourself on the back, young mother, and keep your head high
You are the true Superhero

I'm the LIFE of the Party

To know me is to know that I am one of the most eclectic, eccentric, boisterous, not a care in the world kind of people. My overall personality is the "life of the party" everywhere I go, whether it was the library or a bar mitzvah. I was always the "fun turn up friend." My daily night life routine when I was in my 20s was always one to remember. I had literally been to every club in New York City before I turned 21, thanks to my sister who used to sleep like she was hibernating. I would sneak into her room and steal her ID, or should I say, temporarily borrow. Hey, I always brought it back! I used to party literally every day of the week, the memorable moments interacting with my friends, seducing club promoters and security to get in (which always worked), you name it! My friends and family say I have the "gift of gab;" I could talk my way into and out of anything! I never paid for anything because my conversation got us in places, drinks, and even rides home. I had some moments that I can't even discuss and will take to the grave, but overall, I always made sure we had a good time.

As I step in the club they know my name
Sally from the Valley
Red lipstick
4.5 inch heels
Dress accentuates my tiny curves
They're all watching as I grace them with my presence
I kick my shoes off and dance all over the VIP section
Table tops and stages
Getting Me Bodied to Dutty Wining
Tequila running through my veins
As the DJ shouts me out, I dance harder
Crawling like a Siamese cat on the couches
Exuding my inner sexual beast as the men watch and get turned on
I enjoy every minute of entertaining them
The Ballers pouring that Grey Goose bottle into mouth

It's 4 a.m. and we're still dancing as the wolves continue to howl endlessly
We dance until the sun cracked open the sky
Drunk in love with our own identity
Hair soaked and feet burning
Stumbelinas on the prowl
Driving and drinking like the ignorant bitches we are
Living dangerously cause that's what the LIFE of the party does
Putting our very own lives on the line for a temporary good time
Night after night
Under 21 looking like we're 25
Doing 90 on the Westside Highway
Pissing in the middle of the NYC streets
We are lost to what really matters
We embrace the culture of being all the way turnt up
Entertaining conversations with men we would never see again
What happens in the club stays in the club
That was our motto, the promise we made to each other
Risking a lot to be seen for a few hours of fame with no fortune
Mission accomplished
Waking up with vomit on our underwear
Drinking Gatorades to suppress the hangovers
Phone calls from strangers we met the night before
Putting on a different dialect so they believe they have the wrong number
We then call each other and laugh
We set up a meeting point
Sally gets her gear and heads out
In preparation to do it all over again
Because I'm the LIFE of the party

He/She

There was a season in my life where I battled with homosexuality. During one of those moments, I was caught in a love triangle where I didn't know whether I wanted to be with men or women. I had a very close friend profess her love to me and we began to become intimate. I was confused, lost, and would play both fences. Being Christian, I was so torn because it goes against everything I was taught to believe, but by the same token, love is love. I didn't want to tell my male lover the truth because I knew it would hurt him, so I had to choose between her and him but most importantly my preference. I chose to stay with him.

Her smile, her poise, her presence
The attention she grabs when she enters a room
The strength she possesses
Combatting and conquering the obstacles of today
Embracing the mysteries of tomorrow
The fighter in her and the gentleness that resides in her heart
Limitless love that exudes from her soul
Liberation
The freedom I feel when I'm with her
No comparison with him
We understood each other
Our hearts' desire was so intense
We were happy
There was one question that tormented my mind
Was she the one?
Was this it for me?
I fought with myself daily
Soul to emotion
Heart to mind
I knew what was wrong though it felt so right

I pushed you away
Into the deepest, darkest places of my being
An endless, bottomless pit
Secrets don't come out unless you expose them
I'd rather be tormented and get an internal thrill,
Looking at how beautiful she looks than to actually approach her
Continue to let my fantasies eat at my flesh
And continue to love him

Silent Goodbye

This particular topic is very hard to open up about as it is very personal and sensitive to me. I'm crying as I even write this. I've always been afraid to speak up about this, but I have to for the sake of all women who have hidden this behind closed doors and haven't had an outlet to vent. I had four abortions in my life, and I regret every single one of them. The process of my experiences of taking a life is more traumatic than I could ever explain. I can't even begin to explain the guilt and shame I live with every single day. I can never ask God to forgive me enough, and I know one day I will have to endure the consequences of my actions. So many women go through this process, and people think it's an easy thing to do. For me, it was treacherous, and I hate myself for it. I made mistakes which led up to that, and I don't blame the child for my decisions; however, I did not feel right bringing a child into this world when I could not provide for them. I was barely making it happen for myself. Please know Queen, I am here, and I understand.

As we all wait
Singles and couples
We argue over what will change our lives forever
Either way we will lose this battle
So why not take the easy way out?
Trying to build a mansion out of sand
And so it begins...
The nurse comes and your name is called
It's a long hallway
As you walk toward the empty room of numbness
you begin to see the cloud follow you
You're suffocating
They talk to you
Give you other alternatives
Consider adoption
No

You decline and gracefully get escorted to what is expected to come
They ask more questions
The needle is now in your arm
You decline hearing the heartbeat
Or even seeing the visual of what could have been
In a cold, dreary room full of lost souls,
Trying to find the same door you're yearning for
Blue gown, fuzzy socks, and a name tag, no undergarments
Bare before God and the Devil
For once we all are in one accord as we wait
Hoping we awaken to breathe again
Praying for no complications
Instead of being cleansed of this stain that is embedded in our souls
Murderer!
Though we've made the decision to end a heart that beats within
Some are crying, others itching to go smoke bud, some have blank stares
They call your name
It's time
As you get up
You glimpse over to a woman in her second trimester
You hesitate
How could she take the life of one who already has limbs?
Doesn't matter anymore, and you're not so different
I keep walking
My palms are past sweaty
I desperately try to catch my breath
As the Devil holds my hand and walks me towards freedom again
I lie on the table
Legs open
Just as they insert my dream
I scream, "Wait, I can't do it!"
I fall into the only dream that can keep me calm
Eyes open to only see cracked ceilings and pain
I slowly get up to drink the apple juice and swallow a pill
What could have lasted for eternity I took away in 15 minutes
Impregnated with the guilt that still runs through my veins
I stand waiting for judgment, and I fully embrace what may come

KITTY

There was a season in my life where I became an artist and was being developed as a recording artist. I was with an Independent Record label called "Thorough Records," who I consider family till this very day, despite us going our separate ways. I had stopped writing for a long period of time, but I always wrote my feelings down. During Artist Development, I had reignited that fire and began writing again. It actually helped me develop more things as a writer that I never realized I had inside of me. I wrote a song, which was the first rap song I've ever written by myself. As an independent artist, I was trying to find myself, and as I learned throughout my life, writing was a major outlet for me. I dealt with my pain and my struggles through writing as I wasn't comfortable with speaking about it aloud. I remember listening to Lil' Kim and Nicki Minaj who were pieces of my inspiration behind my writing. This song in particular, I wrote when I was working at Cablevision as a customer service representative and I was listening to Lil' Kim songs on repeat to get the vibe and mood I needed. She definitely allowed me to become comfortable talking about my addiction to sex that I battled with for so long, in addition to the encounters I had with men I had dated and used as boy toys.

Caramel bone eat me down to the gristle
Seductive sex symbol
Blow my kitty off like a whistle
Put it in your mouth and cock it back like a pistol
Kitty got you crying
"Maralyn, I missed you."
Kitty never got an issue so a bitch don't need a tissue
I'm as hard as it gets
Desert dry or soaking wet
Kittyfied sexy
No other bitches next to me
Though they might test me
Freeze them bitches in a hefty

Bad bitch got it made
Sponsors never throw shade
Got 401k and Pensions already paid
Said he love my kitty cushy, smooth not bushy
Droppin' stacks on ya girl
Never fucked he just sucked my pussy
I'm rockin' like a hard dick
Tongue playing pitty pat on my kitty kat
Cause my kitty never slacked
One taste of my kitty kitty
Have you droppin' diamonds and stacks
What cha know about that?

Pull my hair hold me down while you slappin' it up
Like a snake on a mouse my kitty wrapping you up
Jock strap tight like a stripper lapping you up
Once you step into my Kitty zone, baby it's on
Passport stamped international Kitty
Never worried what the next nigga doing for me
Can't help it if my kitty bring the dogs to the big city
Kitty got that wet wet made a nigga sweat
Like playing scrabble on my kitty time to brainstorm
"Daddy you like it ice cold or lukewarm?"
Make a hard porno flicky
You be my Prince I'll be your Nicky
Denim soaking wet sticky sticky
Japan to Brazil he jockin' my kitty cup
Beast like the FEDS tapping me up
Kitty got different types of hoes in different area codes
They on me tighter than a condom on a male gigolo

Mimi Jessica Parker

People who are in my inner circle know me as Mimi. There are many layers of Melissa De Jesus and Mimi is one of the layers I adore. One of my brothers actually named me this. He said it was because Mimi is free spirited, boisterous, and lives in the moment. In times of sadness and despair, I go to Mimi and lie there with her, and because I am able to go there mentally, she helps me deal with my depression and anxiety. Her love to love and love for others is God sent. She was always an outlet for me and assured me everything was going to be okay. Her freedom not only was conducive for me when I had nothing, but her soul is so captivating and loving. She is that little girl that can never go away.

She walks with authority
Her smile radiates a room
Her aura captivates endless souls
Tutu skirt and stilettos
Golden blonde hair prancing on her back
Her hobo sleeps on her shoulder
She embraces those who need uplifting
She encourages those in despair
She is the outlet, freeing to those who are bound
She gives LIFE

Always on the go
She pushes to create legacy
She learns from the greats and builds her own foundation
Nuggets embedded in her caramelized skin
Her life experiences written across her soul
Her selfless love resides in her heart
She is the reflection of a hero
Never idolized
She is inspiration

Living without a care
No worries of tomorrow and living for today's moment
Freedom is her best friend
She is endless
Partying till the sun bathes the sky
She is intoxicated with the love of dancing in the moonlight sun with Abba
She feels alive
As she rocks back and forth to her very own beat
She is in tune with herself
She is accomplished in spite of
She is a Queen
She is Mimi

Play It Back

The process of being an artist is a strenuous one. I commend every artist in the game, hustling trying to make it happen, rising from dust. Just thinking of the sleepless nights, long hours in the studio, constant workouts, strict diets, countless photoshoots, wigs, makeup galore, and the list goes on. Being an artist and being exposed to so much showed me what the industry was really about. The constant exposure and peer pressure from sex, drugs, the forced false images they place on you for great P.R., secrets and lies, fame cravers, selling your soul, you name it! I met Big Homie, who was the wife and Vice President of the record label that I was signed to. We became a family. We had our ups and downs, but I learned a lot about myself and this industry because of her. My goal was to always inspire, spread love and motivation to women. To love who they were and be confident with their inner selves. I never had anyone to chisel me and show me how to love myself and be okay with who I was and my mistakes. I soon learned that those people closest to you were the vultures waiting to devour you in any way possible.

Lights, camera, action
You yearned to be seen
I was your token to opening that door
Sexual in every way
Arrogant and confident
The 5 Star Diva of every man's dream
From Kitty to Play It Back
Working day and night to get the sound right
Anxious to grace the stage with her presence
She became addicted
It consumed her
Even when the inappropriate touch invaded her territory
Comments about what they thought of her made it hard to work with them
She lied and entertained it
She had one common goal

To be famous by being herself
To push even if it meant bleeding out to get to the top
Releasing her pain through song and being able to dance freely about it
Opening up the very doors she was always afraid to open to someone
Her addiction allowed her to be carefree
No matter if she had to push up her breasts and let a cheek hang
She was down for it
As uncomfortable as it made her
She cherished the bond she had with them
She became Maralyn, the sexual predator
She was willing to go above and beyond to make her Big Homie happy
She wanted them to accept her
As we charted #1 on the Billboards
The hopes of performing at the MTV Awards
Even if it meant losing precious moments of seeing her son grow
She was willing to sacrifice for everyone's sake
Sleepless nights, studio runs for days, and endless backyard rehearsals
Her body began to defeat itself
She pressed on even when the bruises became noticeable
He knew exactly what she wanted and gave it to her
The more she dug, the deeper she fell in
Fame was now embedded into her skin
There was no escape
She would do anything for them, even if it meant losing herself
She was now the product of a brand she didn't sign up for
As it began to suffocate her to the point of gasping for air
The only thing she could do is run and never return
So she ran and left it all behind to find the pieces of herself that was left

Just Friends

"Friends with benefits" is the new thing now during this day and age. People don't believe in monogamy anymore, which is so sad. Being "Just Friends" was just as potent way back when, but people wore it so much better. What gets me is how women claim they can handle it, but they really can't separate their feelings from what they came to do. It is in our innate nature to have emotions the way we do. I was one of those women. I was dealing with someone who wanted to be just friends, but then it got really complicated. There were so many mixed signals in the air, you could breathe better in hell.

Define "Just Friends"
Is it the same to you as it is to me?
From Friday night movie dates to working out two hours straight
Special evening drives
Our temples embraced each other
Flaws and all
The fight that ended us was so big
Didn't care that our "Just Friendship" would fall
And now your ass don't even call
My heart feels bitter, limp, and small
But tell me, is this what "Just Friends" do?

We ate, we laughed, we cried, we shared
Truth of it all, you showed you cared
And though black and blue
My heart was true
But tell me, is this what "Just Friends" do?

Why run away from the words "I love you?"
Don't friends love?
You once said, "What's wrong with being in love with a friend?"
I end up there, you run off scared and said we had to end,
You lived a lie

The daily agenda we once shared
Yeah you showed you really cared
Isn't this the "Just Friends" definition to you?
We swam conjoined through the depths of the oceans
Climbed each other's mountain tops
Devoured each other whole
Yet now our story's hidden, left untold
Your "Just Friend" concept was toxic in my veins.
Venom. Cancer that slowly devoured who I really was
You exposed me, just to slowly watch me decay
While your smile became my addiction
The touch of your skin to mine was my crack
It got too intense
My emotions were under attack
Your words broke me
I was nothing more than your midnight snack
So please let me dare to ask
Is this what "Just Friends" do for you?

How can you have a lover and friend that you know isn't true
Should I have smiled in your face then lie to you?
Or use and abuse the inside of you?
Take you for granted and deny what's true?
Is this the "Just Friend" you want beside you?

Let me ask you something else my love
Is this the "Just Friend" you prayed for to God above?
Is this your view on "Just Friend" love?
I may never hear your voice again
Our morning phone calls saying, "Good Morning Friend"
Because I've accepted this as the end

To our special "Just Friends" short term trend
Though my scars will heal and my heart will mend
I will never have another "Just Friend"
The friend who made me feel, made me hurt
Are shattered pieces of one's broken happiness attempting to mend?
Don't care what you say, this shit was real on my end.

Ice

Have you ever felt so in love it made you numb? You were so stuck and frozen that before you knew it, you came back to your senses and realized everything you thought had evaporated and you had no clue? The feeling and moment when you're in it comes and melts away like ice. How can love evaporate right before us? I believe we all can attest to that kind of love. You never see it coming and in the blink of an eye it's gone, and you don't even know how.

Here it is
You can see right through it
It shows all of its flaws, as transparent as breath
The thought of it on your lips creates the coldest winter ever as it merges together
Yet you embrace it
Your addiction becomes of it
Despite what you may want, the melting will amerce
It is something you may want but can never have
That's how I feel with you

Our love is one big ice block
As bad as I want you to stay
You will eventually melt away
It sucks doesn't it?
Something you want so bad that you know you can never have to hold forever
It melts and eventually evaporates
Your love was a block of ice
I could see right through it
So forever in the freezer you shall remain

Harlem's Favorite Lady

My Aunt/Grandmother Rosland was the adopted sister to my maternal grandmother. She literally was like my grandmother that helped raise me. She was amazing, stern, and strict, yet loving and loved all of us equally as if we were her own. She lived in Harlem and I remember always looking forward to going over there to be with my extended family. Blood couldn't make us any thicker. She taught me a lot about life, hard work, and the importance of never giving up on family. I always admired her strength and the love she gave.

You believed in the importance of a strong knit family
Solid foundation preventing unbreakable roots
As we watch Whitney Houston and Chaka on repeat
Gave every reason to be every woman
We slowly create the memories of forever
Blood couldn't make us any thicker
Family is what you helped give us
Loving us more than we could even imagine
That love now passed on
Forevermore embedded into our souls
Tough exterior couldn't contaminate the warmth you possessed within
Grandma's hands were always on time
To pray for us
To whoop us
To love us
To clean a cut
To encourage us
Constantly dropping wisdom into our souls
Your strength throughout your illness kept us whole
A role model, simple and sassy
Raising us to shine bright as the moonlight
As you dance into forever with the Harlem sky

Interrogation

My ex-fiancé was my knight in shining armor or so I thought. In the beginning, the relationship was amazing and he could do no wrong in my eyes. As time passed, I began to see who he really was. I lived in fear every day and had to be tough in spite of how lonely and afraid I was internally. My son was with me, so I didn't want to fail in his eyes. He sensed a lot, granted he wet the bed and suffered from separation anxiety whenever he wasn't around me. He needed to see a counselor for his unusual behavior, although I knew where it was coming from. I prayed to God for a way out and boy did He give me one! I found out that my ex-fiancé had been accused of rape, and though he won the case, he received a dishonorable discharge and had to leave the military. I later then found out that he had a serious drinking problem and his love for hitting women was a way to express his feelings. I stayed with him in spite of the silent abuse, but every single day I questioned myself constantly as to why I was still there. This wasn't me, and my family had no idea. As time passed, I left his house and got my own. He eventually moved in with me after all his "I'm sorrys" and ways of making it up to me, which was the worst thing I could have done. While I worked full time and went to school full time, I would leave my house as early as 6 a.m. and come home as late as 10 p.m., I was never home. My son would sit outside or inside the classroom with me as I went to night school. I thought that at this point, my ex-fiancé was on track and we would be stronger than ever. But man was I fooled again! I found out after being pulled over by detectives and brought to the precinct that, in addition to bringing women to my home and cheating, my ex-fiancé had been dealing drugs and was having them sent to my house without my knowledge. I almost went to jail for it! I literally had no idea. I went through a process of interrogation, investigation, and I had to pay a lawyer $5,000, which he eventually told me I didn't have to pay anymore, thank God.

I got evicted out of my New Jersey home, lost everything, and had to move back to New York and start all over. To this day, I am paying for things my ex-fiancé and I shared. I was manically depressed, suicidal, and mentally tormented on a daily basis. Every second of that month that this issue transpired, my ex-fiancé was with me, and I had to put on a mask as if everything was okay. I knew he did it; I could feel it. The detectives knew too, they just used the little fish to get to the big fish. I realized he wasn't going to be a man and take the fall after an intense phone call when the police were going to take me and charge me with the drugs. He never came to the police station to come get me after screaming numerous times that he was on his way. He lied and denied it all.

The detectives clearly saw that night, based on the phone call, that I was in the wrong place at the wrong time. They knew it was him. They told me to leave him because no real man would ever put his woman through this. I remember crying silently in the shower every day so my son couldn't hear me and had to wear an "I'm okay" mask so he couldn't see my pain. I couldn't let my ex-fiancé see that I knew what was going on during the investigation. He denied it all. I lost 15-20 pounds and suffered from severe dehydration and almost ended up being admitted to the hospital. Months had passed, and his aunt came to see me to see if I was okay. She admitted that he did do it because his mother had informed her that he was having drugs sent to her house without her consent as well. The only thing I am guilty of is falling in love with a man that had a secret life, and it almost cost me my son being taken away, my freedom, and my life.

The room is small
Black
Dark
Waiting patiently
They offer water
You accept
Your child eats pizza and watches cartoons
You wait
In this little black room
Empty
Your soul has checked out
Numb
No possibility of tomorrow
Indulging in conversation that seems off, intense
They misunderstand you
Naïve and blind to their goal
You did nothing wrong
You just wanted to get food at a local church pantry for your child
He put you in a situation of no hope

No freedom
Transforming into an animal in the system
Uncle Sam will be your child's provider
You ask them why, as your heart is sprinting
Palms Sweaty
As you drown trying to grip the truth
Pushing to catch your breath
Answer after answer
Knowing you were innocent
Yet they prey on you like fresh meat
You know nothing
An unknown box that is not yours
A good Samaritan
A funny feeling
You try to do the right thing
You become prey
You give them all you have
You now see the one you love as the one who tried to bury you alive
He drowns you
In this very dark room
Full of endless silence
As your emotions boil through your veins
You scream and break to pieces
Is this little dark room called interrogation?
Full of anxiety
Sorrow
Anguish
The detective tapping his pen on the table
The voices come into your head
You're innocent
You knew nothing
Six excruciating hours
They let you go
You drive home
In complete silence
Knowing this is only the beginning

I Waited

We as women have a tendency to settle for men that are not 100 percent ready or properly equipped to be with a woman. So we wait with the hope that one day they will be the man we need them to be. In spite of their flaws, we sit and deal with the cheating, the neglect, the lack of communication, the dismissive behavior as if we are not good enough, hell, all the way down to the abuse. My relationship with my ex-fiancé, though we had great times (in the beginning), overall was abusive. He was a functioning alcoholic and dealt drugs. He manipulated me and it almost cost me my life. I was at a low point in my life where I was afraid, yet I tried to show strength though he knew that I was vulnerable. He used that to keep control over me for approximately four years until I eventually found a way out for myself and my son. He moved me to another state where I had no family, but I was so excited and in love, so I dismissed all the signs of abuse. I disconnected from my family and friends and turned into a totally different person. I waited for him to be my Prince Charming when all he ever was was a toad. The only thing I was ever guilty of was loving the wrong man and waiting for a hopeless fairy tale. My last poem "Interrogation," gives more of a description as to what happened during this relationship. I waited for a grown-ass boy to become a grown-ass man. I believed in potential as opposed to believing in who he really was.

You said I could trust you
Your dream was to hold my heart, ever so sore
Trusting you, I opened the door
Entire being was yours
Excited for our future
I waited

Times looked rough
But you're tough
I am too

Even through the black and blue
Money low, cheating grew
Promising me anew
Yet you still held my heart
So, I couldn't part
Laying down dismay
Praying, hoping one day
So I waited

Drinking out of control
Defecate on my soul
Still I tried to grab hold
Of our tomorrow
I was promised from the start
And I gave you my heart
Now you're full of sorrys and change
So I stayed
and I waited

I waited in the blistering cold
Not a hat or a glove
Thin socks, bare on rocks
I waited

Fiddling my thumbs
As my toes become numb
Brain of books, then to dumb
I waited

Bloodshot red hit the floor
As the wolves come, galore
Panting hard, lungs get sore
I waited

Frozen tears on my side
Fear can no longer hide
Death has stolen my pride
I waited

Heads now one with the floor
Strength has fled out the door
Nothing left no amor
I left

His Blood

As a minority female growing up in areas where poverty was my roommate, I was exposed to and experienced my share of racism, civil disobedience, and police brutality. This definitely was not uncommon. So every day you left home, you had the mentality that this may be your last day kissing your mother, laughing with your siblings, taking a warm shower in the bathroom, or lying in your bed looking at the glow in the dark stars you taped on the ceilings. You would constantly see the police harassing us for no apparent reason, the intimidation, stopping and frisking young men and even women in the public streets, exposing their genitals out in the open, stripping them, emasculating them as if we were in slavery. It was the modern-day back-breaking technique they used to instill fear and torment, and keep us afraid and put us in cages like wild animals. It was either jail or death when it came to the authorities.

He lays on the floor
Lifeless
No more panting
His heart drums a final tune
Hoping that he is now in the hands of the Lord
As your emotions prepare to sing
The numbness of your soul compresses the explosion
This innocent yet lifeless soul will now be labeled
The young Black man that was killed
Due to the injustices of the America we live in
The same America for which ancestors before us have fought and gave their lives
The cotton that was picked by the bloody hands of our forefathers
Countless rapes and tireless hours serving the ignorant
Who refused to see the beauty we possessed.
Fear in our eyes as we lived trapped in the struggle

Countless tears shed for those you gave birth to being sold and never seen again
Harriet Tubman being a light for those who risk their lives for the freedom
To smell the fresh cut grass as the sun awakens without being killed over it.
A harmless young brother being thirsty after a very long day of school,
Can't drink water from the same fountain
To the memories you try to capture with your loved ones,
Can't share forks in the same restaurant as those who have no pigment
Crying as you beg for mercy watching your fathers and brothers carried away
Bodies after bodies from riots fighting for equality.
Giving birth to pigment-free men
Who use racial slurs as the only weapon he has
Due to his own fear of what he was taught
Rosa Parks wanting to go home so she sits in a nameless seat
To the very marches of Dr. King with the hopes that love can overcome hate
Malcolm X and Black Panther frustration as they finally reach the cap of non-violence,
Using violence to get their points across.
From the hoodie that played the main character that ended Trayvon Martin's life
To the cigarettes that led to Eric Garner's very last breath
Becoming one with the cold concrete
As Trump sits high and directly verbalizes
His true feelings on how he sees Black America
He is the reflection of what our America has been and always was
The past of ignorance just wore their stripes of racism differently
If you could only see what's inside of us beyond the blood
His blood was too black to see that he was human just like you
He is the same as you, just created with a different texture
When will his blood stop shedding?!
When will my heart stop being minced?!
When will you see what his blood really has to offer this world?
You smile in the faces of his blood
When he makes you millions off music and sports
You stand next to his blood
When he builds your empires
You'll break bread with his blood
When he has ideas or goals providing a better future

You'll profit off of his blood.
But you won't stand up for his blood
When it is on the floor right next to you, screaming and crying for help
All his blood needs is the hand of your support
To stand behind him and fight for him through the toughest time in his life
The time when change is the only way
You can break that cycle
But pride has consumed your being, so you sleep with eternal shame
You know there is injustice yet you do nothing
You can't praise him in public because you bash him in private
You're the kind of racist that has no idea he is.
So, without further ado, let me ask this question to you
What will you do when one day your blood will be the cause of his too?

Heaven

My relationship with God has always been a unique one. The kind of relationship people will never understand. When God shows me something, it has to be so dramatic due to my severe hardheadedness lol. Throughout all I have ever endured, I always found a way to escape the madness and speak to Abba (as I call Him), getting away from my sorrows. These are just some descriptions of my most intimate encounters with God. He was always my escape. I remember beaches being my quiet place to commune with Him, one of the most intimate places I would go just to cry, laugh, think, and pray. I remember my family going to Orchard Beach as a child, and being happy in that moment before all the storms came to shore. It was always our family's safe haven, and it is mine until this very day.

I've always wondered how heaven would be
Soft clouds, Angels dancing throughout eternity
Wheat cascading with wind, a sunset scenery
We laugh at everything

We run on a beach as the sun smiles gently on our skin
Laughing at the endless waves
Staring into the eternal ocean where love dwells forevermore

We stand together under one umbrella in the rain
You wipe the dripping water from my face
I slowly look into your eyes
Sharing an intimacy that only a creator shares with His creation
A peaceful, graceful admiration
The rain touches the ground, yet we remain dry
Laughing as we gaze into each other's souls

Maybe that is what heaven is
Just an eternal imaginative moment where time is timeless
I wake up into reality as I worship, and I realize I want to go back
To the heaven you showed me, while my flesh graced the earth
I will wait for you until you return

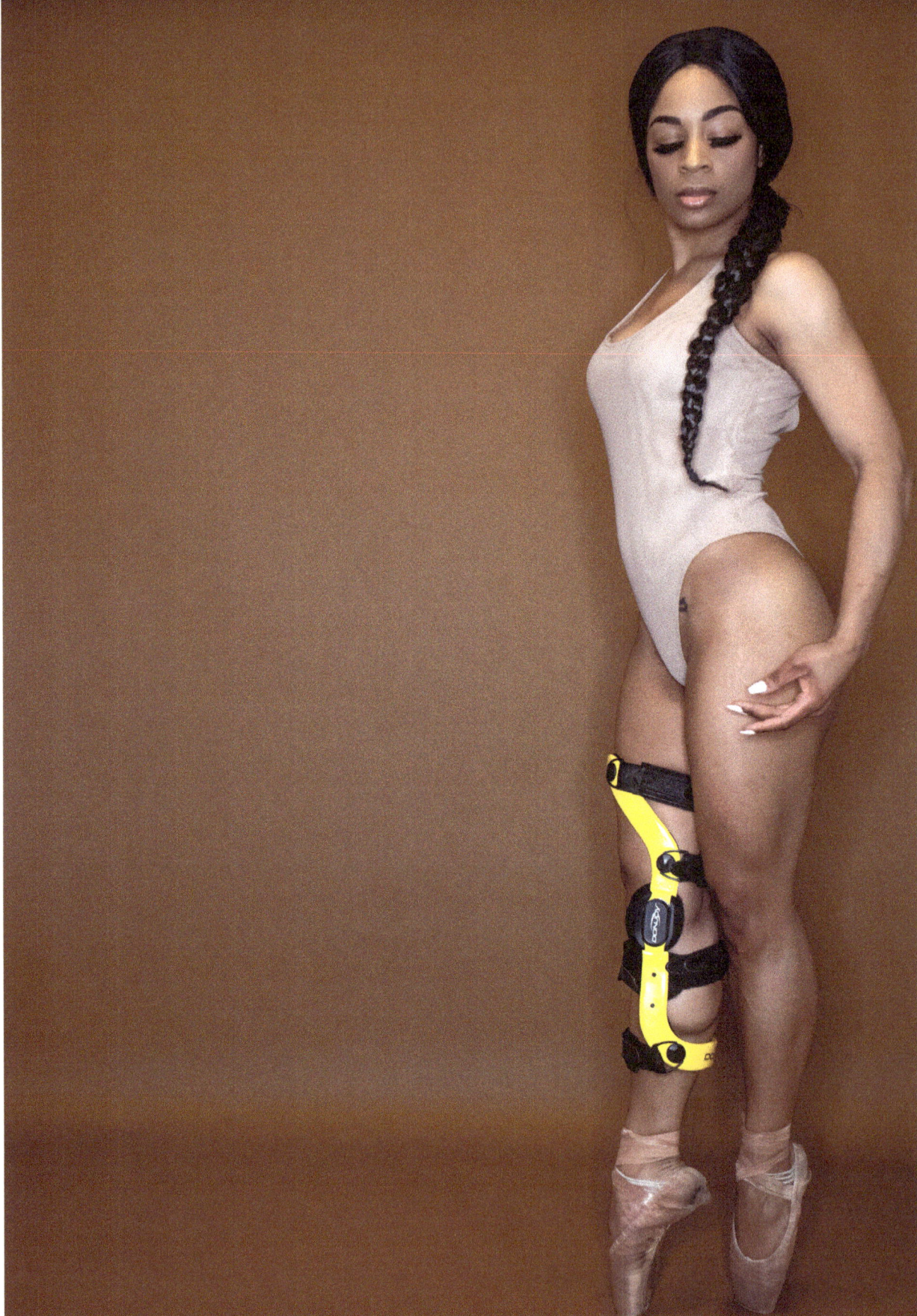

Dolly Bumblebee

I severed my ACL and had to get emergency surgery to repair it. I vividly remember my emotional state; feeling hopeless and worthless as if I couldn't go on, especially being a single parent and having all the heat on me. It was like dominoes, once one fell everything fell out of place. It was an extremely traumatic time in which having to show your body how to work again was trying. Like an adult learning to walk all over again. I lost my job because of this accident. As a single mother, it was so hard to take care of my son, and it got to the point where I had to pay my family just to support me and help me take care of him. The mental recovery process was so much worse than the physical.

As traumatizing as it was, it also was a rebirth for me. I remember being in the park sitting with my crutches. A guy came up to me and we began talking as if we had known each other for years. He told me how he was a recovered drug addict, being clean for 5 years and counting. He elaborated about one special meeting that changed his life. He discovered a way to help him get through this dark time, to not relapse but instead to look at the future and the light at the end of the tunnel. He chose everyday to wear a color that's vibrant so that when he feels he is in that dark place again, he looks at that color and he is reminded where the light at the end of the tunnel is. He went on to explain how he named the color and would sing about the color.

I eventually had to wear a leg brace after my surgery until I had full range of motion. I was able to choose the color of my brace and I chose my favorite color, which was also bright, to help me. I chose yellow. I named my brace Dolly Bumblebee; Louis Armstrong is one of my favorite singers and Bumblebees are yellow, plus I would watch Tyler Perry and Transformers all the time during my recovery phase (lol). Everytime I felt discouraged and was going into that dark place, I looked at that color and sang Hello Dolly and was reminded of the light at the end of the tunnel. I remembered my resilience and the strength I had and couldn't see. Dolly was my reminder that I would heal in more ways than I'd even realized.

Stealing the attention of strangers
As you entered any room
Dressed in a smooth sleek canary yellow finish
Completing and comforting what was left of me
Each strap holding me tighter
She comforts me beyond any relief.
She was my getaway when the pain invaded my flesh
I could barely speak or eat
She was my peace

Afraid to look into the mirror and see the new me
Gazing into the new instrument
Helping me learn to walk again
Pondering in advance my bathroom trips
Its comfort left me insecure
I remained a clam to what new possibilities this surgery had to offer
Seeing only abandonment, pain, and eternal scars
The very legs that made its mark on this earth have been destroyed
I now sit in a room full of snakes
Acting as if they cared for my recovery yet silently praised for my demise
I could feel their scaly skin rub up against mine
Adding more discomfort to what already lies
I pray
As I sit in church wondering why God would do such a thing to me
I blamed myself for dancing with broken people
I blamed myself for not seeing the signs
Going over the accident piece by piece, over and over in my head
I am a professional who was trained by the greats
I blame myself
What could I have done to prevent this
With a bedpan and Percocet,
I watch Tyler Perry's production on the crucifixion of Jesus Christ
I soak in my sorrows and depression creeps in
I say to myself, "How could Jesus have endured such pain and not given up?"
I then look at my situation as a process to progress
As weird as it may sound,
Maybe God was giving me a new walk, a new dance
I tried, and as much as I wanted to just give up, I couldn't

Jesus had his flesh literally ripped off of his bones,
Holding his head high on that cross.
There was no excuse
Though I wanted to throw all my gifts in the garbage and walk away normal
God wouldn't let me
So I then began to hold my head high with the help of Dolly
She pushed me to go forward
She became my catalyst
With every squat, lunge after lunge
Bending and stretching, turning and running
Dolly was right there
Her vibrancy always rejuvenated what was running on E
She recharged the emotions that ran out of control
When I couldn't see past the process
Hip to skin
Tear to pore
She was my freedom in times of despair

Church Hurt

My time in the "Black Church" was one of the worst times, worshipping God in spite of the smiles I had to put on. It amazes me how some Black people can treat others yet profess they love God and His people. Keep in mind I said "some." From the lies, deceit, and hatred placed on me, it turned me away from seeing God for who He was. The cult-like customs and how they perceive the Bible made me believe God would never accept me. They made you believe if you're not screaming loud enough, God is not going to hear or accept your praise. I know not all Black churches are like that, but their presentation would make you believe all churches were the same. I was ridiculed, mistreated, and casted away for not only the person I was dating, but because they saw my gifts and what my gifts could do, and envied it. If you weren't a favorite, you were exiled and overlooked. It hurt so bad that I remember going to church with weapons to harm people. God always dealt with me as I didn't want to be like them. I could never comprehend how evil some of God's people can really be and how those people push away others who really need God and are bleeding their lives away. People really come to church hurt and in need of help. The church is supposed to be the hospital and we are supposed to be the medical staff helping care for them as they go through the healing process as God is the Doctor. It irks me how we constantly beg for money and people give their last, their rent and bill money with the belief that God will turn it around, and we abuse and mistreat those same loyal people. It would make you believe this is what we are to endure. Church hurt is beyond real.

I lift my hands to you in pure worship
As they stare and laugh
Silent conversations and speculation
Intimidation is their foundation
They work diligently to destroy mine
Swallowing my pride, I try to make wrongs right
Though I am not to blame
Piercing words that cause me to bleed to death

I lose my breath
My lungs are collapsing
Trying to fight, drowning in my own blood
I become fatigued
They stand, watch, stare
They talk, yet provide no resolve
Speak lies that torture my soul
I become numb
Isn't this supposed to be the hospital?
Your rotation is only killing me
As I lay in the Intensive Care Unit
I realize
We are no longer the same heartbeat
Though we come from different walks of life
I continue to push in spite of the hurt and sorrow
Like a bullet slowly pushing its way through the crevasses of my heart
The silent breakdown invades my entire being
Seeking God in an empty space
He is omnipresent, however I checked out
Push to seek His face Mel, you can do this
With God, all things are possible
Or what about I'M-Possible?
When the war scars become infected
The time has come to dismember my body
So the infection doesn't fester
It's too late
Where the love I once had resides
Where the God I know once dwelled
I am broken beyond repair
My shattered glass will cut Him
So therefore He has to leave
Where is the light when I really need it?
I can't see it
I am alone
They put me there
As I seek counsel from the Pastor
As the Elders pray and fast for me
As the ministers and deacons serve me Holy Communion

I can't get past the fact that they hurt me to the core
They looked the other way
They lied on me through the deception of their actions
As they try to restore the wounds with the same salt they used to create them
I can no longer see the God they were supposed to emulate
I no longer see the God in me
I no longer see God
I no longer see

Shelter Who?

My son and I were homeless for an extensive period of time. We went from house to house for a while, but eventually it came to a point where the Lord was leading me to enter the Shelter system. After losing everything yet still being a full-time student in college and my son still being a full scholarship recipient with Alvin Ailey Dance School, we juggled a lot trying to keep our sanity afloat. It was one of the hardest decisions I've ever made in my life, however one of the best. Despite the poor and hazardous conditions, rodents all over the place, mold on the walls, the angry and disrespectful social workers and staff that belittle and talk down to you constantly, this situation helped me get back on my feet. Although being in that situation humbled me to the core, I learned to depend on me again. I also learned that the system is debilitating; the social workers and staff are discouraging through their constant belittlement, nasty attitudes, and lack of efficiency for getting your affairs in order, which they are paid to do. It makes you believe that they don't want to see you win. They automatically believe you are some poor welfare case. I graduated from college as I walked across the Madison Square Garden stage to receive my degree while living in the shelter. I got a promotion at work and my son was excelling in school while dancing as a scholarship student at Alvin Ailey. They looked at me as if I was dirt, but when they saw my stats, they began to speak to me differently and saw a rose who was rising expeditiously in the dust.

(12/10/2016, Winter Time, New York City)

You sit,
You wait,
Fingers fiddle,
Heart racing past your thoughts,
The unknown,
You panic,
You're Angry,

You contemplate
You doubt,
The shame
Believing you're fighting the system when the battle is really within,
Over 12 hours waiting on a process that could have been expedited,
You're placed.

It's 1 a.m.,
For the first time in my life,
This train ride is a foreign one,
As he sleeps on my shoulder,
Tears silently fall down my cheeks,
The same cheeks that once shaped a smile.
Here I am,
This is my life now,
Feeling so worthless,
Feeling worse than death itself.
What kind of mother am I?
Who is this woman?
Where did it all go wrong?
How did I get here?
As I stand before this new journey,
I contemplate that NOW I can really relate.

Cracked floors,
Roaches reside along my bedside,
Afraid yet having to stand strong for him,
He is watching my every move,
Push harder,
Don't sweat,
Do not fall even if you're slipping,
As they belittle you,
As they create surly conversations,
The light shines on my reality,
I'm worthless to them,
Suffocating me with disrespect towards everything I am,
I never asked to be here,
Yet your lack of empathy contaminates my despair,

There is nothing left in me.

As I lay down on a twin-size bed,
As the screams of the children attack my dreams,
As the desperate, depressed, angry, bitter women
Verbally and physically abuse the innocent,
With forever words that scar souls,
All I can do is cry a very dry, dark cry.
All I can do is lay there and weep.
Please leave me alone.
I isolate myself,
Unsure of what door to walk through,
Imagine doors surrounding you in a circle,
One of them in flames,
The other drenched in thorns,
Another drowning in a never-ending ocean,
Lost at which one to choose,
Either way you will lose,
Numb,
You hope God's plan will be accomplished
In spite of fearing what's ahead,
The unknown,
Eyes wide shut yet open,
Who will save me?

Sharing the same sadness and depression as the days go by,
Secretly creeps upon you,
Hits you when you least expect it,
You're ravaged,
Raped from your sanity,
Your happiness,
A hopeless soul,
A slave to statistics,
Powerless, defeated,
Yet you're able to put your pride aside to save your seed,
I am visibly homeless yet you don't see me,
You can't fathom my pain, my sorrow,
Because you believe your promise is today,

Yet you're not guaranteed tomorrow,
Like a thousand pieces of shattered glass,
You have now broken me beyond repair,
Tried picking my own self up,
The pieces only deepen the wounds,
Without intent,
I am dying from my own brokenness
That people failed to want to save,
Failed to care to save,
As I bleed profusely,
As you watch and do nothing,
As you control my future with your emotionless actions,
Without me,
It is impossible to be you,
And the seeds you plant in my garden of life are also planted in yours too

1118

During your experience in the Shelter system, you see a lot and you hear a lot. Behind closed doors, it was a totally different world when the lights went out. The haunting things you see, hear, and experience in the night when you think people are asleep, haunt me till this day. From the abuse from parent to child, domestic disputes between parents, the weird demon-like sounds and psychotic laughs, crying, and yelling from people in despair and feeling sorrowful at night, it was a haunting memory that sticks in your soul and stays with you forevermore.

As I gazed down the hallway
To my left
To my right
Eight doors are planted
Dressed in powder blue
Cracked and unpolished
Each represented human life
The handy worker
The innocent
The bitter insecure woman
And me
1118
You could smell the fear and sadness exuding through each door
As the secretions drip
Staining the soul who resides beyond the entrapment of loneliness
As I stare and ponder
What could be going on on the other side of that door
From hearing the cries of hunger
To the screams that cry out sorrow
To the profanity birthed by a learned behavior
I then lose my breath and shut my door
I then ponder no more

St. Mary's Angel in Disguise

As a child, my fraternal grandmother was more present in my life before my parents' divorce. Once they divorced, my father literally divorced us. So we didn't get to see my grandparents the way we would have wanted to. I would have given anything to have had a closer relationship with her than the one I had. Though it was great and intimate, I always wanted more. She taught me so much about God and was the reason I follow and love God the way I do today. She taught me how to love as if I have never been hurt before and taught me the true meaning of forgiveness. Her constant prayers for us proved that she was an angel that protected us in spite of.

She was the epitome of what God's reflection mirrored
She understood life and accepted the cards she was dealt
Without hesitation and without regret
She saw the abuse and helped protect the innocent
She saw the neglected and suffocated them with love
She saw the heart
And everything it had to give
So, she gave everything
Because God is love she dedicated her life to emulating that
Creating a mosaic of generations as we enter her place of peace
Pictures and statues complete what resides in her heart
Showing us her reflection
Her grace was like a butterfly who just received its wings
No matter how much time it took to adjust to know how to fly, she waited
Ever so patiently
Her wisdom was as pure as the garden of Eden
With every embrace

With every kiss
Though worry pondered from time to time,
Tried its best to contaminate her thoughts
She always knew we were in the hands of God,
And God was her greatest power
Her secret yet exposed weapon
So she feared not
Her confidence with who she served inspired me to become one with Him
She is the reason I am here today
A grandmother's prayer moves mountains,
Shakes the very fear that corrupted one's mind
It destroys the plans of all evil
It gives birth to a blank canvas,
We can create our own story through the lens of God
It plants seeds for tomorrow.
And she did just that.
She planted seeds in all of us
Though she may not be around to see the fruit manifest
She will always be with us in our hearts
So therefore, she will see God's reflection through us
She will see her prayers come to life
Because she is us
And we are her

Had to Let You Go

I never enjoyed having to let someone go. Though you may want a person to come with you on your journey, God has other plans. Sometimes it's really hard to let someone you love go, but even though you love them, it does not mean they are meant for you. I remember having to let people go even though I tried so hard to keep them on my journey; it was God saying they are not to continue with you. I had to put on my big girl panties and move on.

We come from two different worlds
Desperately seeking the same face
Trying to find love
Hoping we find it in each other
Hoping to dance conjoined for all eternity
Looking past our life, holding hands
Seeing our children and grandchildren play, sing, and dance
We embrace each other's hearts as one
We are grateful
Legacy fulfilled
Though we didn't begin one

Doing their best to sever what we had
With their lies and assumptions
It worked
I bleed before you
As you try to close wounds with your bare hands
You begin to bleed
We fail
Misunderstood
Communication was not there
We drown

Hopeless
Having nothing left to give each other
Only love, we thought we sought to fight for

I let you go
For your own sanity
For my own identity
For our hopeful eternity
I may never hold your hand
Filled with the memories of tomorrow
I may never smile and watch you sleep as the sun opens its heart to us
I may never get to bring your legacy into this world
It hurts indeed
But not as bad as me contaminating who you are
What you stand for
So, I had to let you go
God makes no mistakes
I try my best to believe
I need to work on the inner me
My happiness
I was unhappy
My light dimmed and I couldn't let yours too
So I cut the rope forever on loving you
I had to let you go

CNM: Godsfavour
RN: Micaela
PCA:
BA: Jorge
KP4: rm 435B
Friday, March 17, 2017

Blood Clot NOT

I was rushed to the Emergency Room after an abnormal test showed I had multiple PE (pulmonary embolisms), also known as blood clots, in my right lung. Praying to God so hard while waiting in the Emergency Room, I was admitted and was taken to a room where I would be given medications to hopefully make the blood clots disappear. That night I became a miracle child. I was awakened by the doctors as they asked me what was the last thing I remembered being told. The first thing I said in my head was, "God, what did you do?" I then proceeded to inform them what I had been told regarding the second series of tests that confirmed the blood clots in my right lung. According to their records, after they said that they had to reconfirm some things and redo tests, they all came back negative. They couldn't explain how, but I told them I knew it was Jesus. The doctors told me how many down to the size of them. I remember looking into my room name. On the board they write your name, the nurse's name, and additional information so they can identify who you are, but my information said "God's Favour." That has never happened in a room in that hospital. I know because I worked in that hospital on countless units and have never seen that before. I remember one of the last prayers that night asking God to remember me as He remembered Sampson that one last time and gave him the strength to destroy the temple. I was that Sampson, and I am forever grateful for this miracle.

Headaches
Dizziness
Shortness of breath
Swollen legs
Chest pains kept me up at night
I kept going with the insomnia that invaded my territory
Am I dying?
Weeks go by,
I can't take this feeling my body is screaming out to me,

I ignore it
I finally take the step to go see a doctor
Hours later the call comes in
I rush to the ER
As I walk to flag a cab I call my immediate family
In the event that I die
Keep KJ in Ailey, teach him the things I wasn't able to teach him
Let him be who Abba has called him to be
As my heart pants and I sweat in the green taxi
I call my friend for prayer
Tears roll down my cheeks and become one with the sweat.
I remain centered because Abba is my true doctor.
In the Emergency Room
I wait
All tests were conducted
Admitted
Multiple blood clots residing in my right lung
I wait
Transporting me to the next phase of what could potentially end my life
I sit in my room alone
Just me and Abba
Crying out to Him
"You didn't bring me this far with all I have lost,
Sacrificed to be obedient and faithful to You.
I know this isn't Your work
I know You would not let me go out from a blood clot!
Lord, remember me!
I'm listening!"
Hours faded into time
I awaken to the sunlight radiating through the window
The doctor comes in and informs me that changes were made overnight
I sit back and calmly ask Abba from my heart,
"What did you do?"
The blood clots they once saw were no more.
Phase 1 demolished.
Abba wins.
Phase 2 required a Doppler test to see if the blood clots were in my legs
I smile, though I am consumed with mixed emotions

The doctors are in awe
They see who the real doctor is
Abba is in control
Phase 2 demolished.
I prepare to go home
I realized my room name was "God's Favour"
I now see the favor of God over my life
To have been healed from what should have taken me out
To be wiped clean of such filth
That should have ended my journey
Cancelled my purpose from progression
I can breathe
I can be a mother
I can be a Director
I can be a Producer
I can be a sister
I can be a friend
I can be a Thithi
I can be a vessel
I can be an inspiration
Because I am HIS
I am a tangible miracle
I can be what wasn't supposed to be

I Am Your Reflection

As a woman evolving and as a mother constantly learning, I finally understand why my mother was the way she was toward me, which resulted in me forgiving her for all I had experienced with her and on my own without her. Realizing that my mother's flaws and faults were learned behaviors that stemmed into fear and other emotions was a pivotal moment for me, especially when I came to realize that I was my mother's reflection. The only thing I ever wanted from my mother was her approval to include me and not treat me like a black sheep. I always felt cast out as if she never wanted me in the first place. All my dreams and work towards reaching my biggest goals was so that one day I could take care of her. I saw her struggles and how she worked hard to keep a roof over our heads, but at the same token, I felt the wrath of how she pushed me away. I came to the realization, after being a single parent myself, that a lot of the mistakes she had made was her doing the best she could with what she had and how she was taught. I had to forgive her, though I didn't like it. I understood so much more, and though we never had a great relationship, I learned how to deal with my mother from a distance, still loving her and caring for her in spite of her ways, because after all, she is my mother, and you only get one mother. I must say I took a vow not to do the things my mom had done to me to my son, to show him love like none other, to root for him, and sacrifice whatever I needed to in order to see him reach his fullest potential. I love my mom dearly, and always will.

From working at the age of 11
Packing bags and braiding hair for six dollars
Frail hands and a big heart
Creating a Christmas that would be remembered
That was the beginning of your reflection in me

Raising six kids alone with a damaged backbone
Doing the best you could with a smile and aching hands
Some things had to suffer so others could remain
With the little you had, you pushed

Recalling the whip lashes from the life you endured
Hips and knees slowly cracking from holding up shattered glass ceilings
Pushing the mountains of life away with your bare hands
In efforts to keep us safe
Standing tall, walking with the strength of a lion
Having the heart of a teddy bear
You've endured the hardest of hardships
Protected your children from the world

The one fight you lost
Was protecting us from ourselves
Anger and no outlets destroyed our foundations
Incoherent and numb to what we really battled with
Using drugs to cope with our true demons
I watch as you sit not knowing what to do
I weep for you
I pray for you

Growing up at a very young age
Helping raise your family
The sorrow of your mother
As her tears fall for your father's passing
I see it was impossible for you to teach me the things I desire
I say to myself you are not to blame
You cannot blame one who does not know or has never been taught
That is when my infected wounds began to heal

Walking face to face with the fears of failing
Yet still walking through my process
I am going to need my mother more than ever
I know that even when you were not around,
The little moments we had shared
The very seeds you planted within me
Have grown into parts of who I am today
The courage you had as a victim of domestic violence
I possess and refuse to let a man walk over me
Your willingness to give was a seed planted within

Selfless to give more than I have beyond my pockets
Your attitude and spice was a seed planted within
People know not to cross me
The gift of creativity God gave to you was a seed planted within
I push in creating art through the arts
Your attempt to keep a broken family mended was a seed planted within
Family is a priority to me
Healing those wounded is the objective

I pray that for the time we have left, we can create those moments
We can create new memories
New reflections we will share
Passing on to the next legacy
Preventing the mistakes, we both made
Creating an enhanced reflection
Breaking the yolk of generational curses
Setting free the stains in our own mirrors
Allowing the reflection of breakthrough to shine through
For I am the reflection of you

Abba

All of my life experiences with God from childhood to adulthood have been such an eye opener. I make mistakes every single day and I am flawed down to the gristle in my bones. The first phase of my life, which I have shared in this book, was so trying that I needed Him to lift me up and get me out of the hole I was slowly dying in. Those of you who feel unworthy and not good enough to get back in His arms, I totally understand your struggle. I was once there and end up there from time to time till this day. That is why God wants a relationship, never mind religion. The more you connect and bond with Him, the more you will gain an understanding of God. He will take care of you, clean up places you thought stained your soul, and make you feel like you are worthy again and always. You are a King/Queen. You are not disqualified. I dedicate this poem to the "unqualified."

Finding me at a place where I embraced the infections that festered,
I adored deteriorating.
Afraid to let go of the known to live for the unknown,
I remained in that familiar fetal position.
You stretch your hands towards me
You join me at my level of brokenness
We stare, we laugh and cry together
Days, months, and years
You never left my side
I trust you
So I give you my hand
You save me
Deliverance

The filth of my decisions has stained my soul
It won't come off
You begin to cleanse me from all impurities
I stare in complete silence

In awe of You
How could someone love me this much?
Taking the time to cleanse my being
As You get dirty
You celebrate
Cleansing the abandoned, used, and abused
Sanitizing all it had to offer me
Ripped to pieces like a dog with a plush toy
I had nothing left to give
You still remained by my side
You cleansed me
Every second, minute, hour
You made a choice
You chose to love me
You chose to stay with me
Even when I left You as the night made love to sin
Seeking my own pleasures
Accepting what the world had to offer
You still cared
You were there
You were patient
Baptism

Your spirit leaves a sweet fragrance
Embedded onto my soul
You see no wrongs
Only the rights that will be
I jump and soar into Your hands
Like a parachute swaying as one with the sky
I remain
Freedom
My flaws evaporate before You
Drifting into the sea of forgetfulness
Without ceasing
I give into intimacy
Creator to creation
The breath You blow into me awakens what's dormant
I am alive.

As we dance towards the eternal sunset
The place where only You and I dwell
I gradually learn the true lessons of life
The importance of the necessary
I endure
I trust the slay
I remain
Long-Suffering

As the wisdom heightens I remain alert and fight
Conforming not to this world
But for the world that's in store for me as I become one with the earth
I transform
Ashes to ashes
Dust to dust

As I build Your kingdom
As opposition attacks from all sides
As the dark creatures serenade themselves with evil into the night
As they methodically plot for my destruction
For my demise
I silently look to the hills and smile
Knowing that no weapon formed against me shall prosper
I then prosper and propel towards my purpose
We soar into a partnership
Because You cared
You were always there
I trust You
As You fight my battles
As I remain still
I hold tight to my faith
To Your promises
As I remain in Your safety
I carve Your name onto my heart
I am married to eternity
I become one with You
I'm no longer afraid
Abba

The Legacy Through Me

Aside from that of God and His creation, there is no better, intimate relationship than that of a mother to child. They grow inside of you, you feel them kicking, the pain you endure as you sacrifice your life for theirs, your souls entwined. You can sense when something is off, their sadness and happiness, all the way down to when they are lying and being sneaky. You realize that this gift is beyond you and God placed them in your hands to care for until it is time for them to go out into the world and pursue their purpose. You are creating the legacy as you are the vessel helping them get there. My son is my legacy, and although I may have had times I didn't get it all right, I tried and still try to be the best mother I can be so that he can carry the mantle after me and bring forth the legacy God has destined for him. Thuthi, this one's for you. I love you!

12:49PM
You arrive
There's no looking back
I cuddle with you as you sleep peacefully
I am beyond afraid
Dancing with my fears of what tomorrow brings
I remember that I am strong
I can do this
I keep pressing
Though doctors suggest braces for your legs
I soak in guilt blaming myself for an assignment beyond my control
The enemy wanted you dead, if not crippled
But God had other plans

Almost choking to death on a chicken bone
My life flashes before my eyes
God was with you once again
Forever thankful

I realize you mean more to me that I can imagine
I protect you with all that I am

You creep, then crawl, then walk
Running into my arms with an organic innocence
I smile to keep from weeping
Daddy makes Mommy sad
Brokenhearted
She can no longer stay, desiring the perfect family
Watched her heart be severed
Having to make a choice before bleeding out
I do what's best for us
I find a safe haven and I protect you
You're now growing up as a fatherless child
I never wanted that for you
Coming into my room and jumping on us on Christmas day
The night of your Senior Prom when your dad is telling me not to overreact
To let you live life
The day we watch you enter your college dorm
Together
Those were my hopes for you
It was my dream for you
To have stability
You were robbed of that chance
Now you have me
And I have you
We're all we have
So we protect each other

Dreamgirls on repeat
You sing and dance
Only three years old
Amazed, so I let you continue to be you
There is something in you I just couldn't put my hands on
Your sense of freedom gives me peace
From worrying about how rent will be paid
The worry of being alone forever
As you grab my face and laugh

You heal the broken pieces in my heart
I am no longer bleeding

Acting and dancing
Play after play
Show after show
You sit in the front
My biggest fan and inspiration
Sitting with strangers as I go on auditions
Sound asleep as I work on scripts
There is little time to be a mom
I neglect you
Yet this is being done for you

I had to make a choice
Lose out on time or an opportunity that will always be there
I run from it all
You in my arms
We go far, far away
I am a ghost in a town full of life
We disappear

A bridge away full of happiness
The water separates us from those we love
We are isolated
Surrounded by lies, witchcraft, and jealousy
I protect you, yet I am the one who really needs protection
You lose focus in school
Internalizing emotions
With no idea of what to do
Disconnecting myself from you
Yet taking care of your needs
You weep silently
Being put in fire
I find an escape for us
We are back in New York

You twitch, squint, and can't control it
It hurts

I hurt
Tourette's
Mind racing a million miles a minute
What will I do?
You get bullied and called gay
My heart is shredded to pieces
I weep for you
Yet you dance anywhere and everywhere
I see there is a way of escape for you
We go to that audition with nothing to lose
As I play worship music sitting silently on the train
Pushing nothing but prayers to God as tears secretly fall down my cheeks
I beg Him to pave a road for you that was better than mine
Creating a way out for you even if it meant leaving me behind
I refused to let my mistakes invade your hopes and dreams
As you walk in a single file line with other children
You look back at me
We share a moment that connected us once again
Spirit to spirit
Son to Mother
Seed to Tree
A legacy was being planted

You're a scholarship student at an elite dance company
You're only ten
Your scholarship remains until your 17th birthday
I see your growth
As I look through the window and watch your freedom come alive in your element
My heart heals
You excel in all you do there
I sit in honor of your accomplishments
I cry tears of joy
Bragging to everyone,
"He is my child
I am proud to call him my son."

From almost being one with death twice
To giving life to everyone you encounter

All I can do is sit back and watch you evolve
The hard work coming into fruition
I take pride in the sacrifices I've made
The choices I had to make
I have no regrets
God has shown me that He was with us all along
In the depths of the rough oceans to the driest of the deserts
With that longsuffering
He created a tangible force
The force I once was
The force I prayed for you to become
You are
My son
My heart
My joy
You are the legacy through me

I Forgive Me

This poem was the hardest poem I've had to write out of all of the poems in this entire book. It is one thing to forgive others for what they may have done to you, but to forgive yourself, it's even harder. I consider this like a "Dear Self" letter, asking myself to forgive me for all the mistakes I've made that I could have prevented had I taken the time to see who I was and what I deserved. I now know that I can't be too hard on myself because those mistakes created lifelong lessons that helped build my character. I had to understand what was meant to destroy me, only allowing discovery unveiling the beauty within my ashes. Allowing myself forgiveness within is merely the beginning steps towards my own healing to help heal others. Pushing to learn to love myself every day and understanding that in this life, we have ups and downs and that is okay. It was never about what you go through in life, but how you handle it. It's about your character, knowing that God has called you to do something while on this earth and with that assignment given, He has to train you by bringing forth battles that will equip you for when the time has come to fully step into your purpose. The future is waiting and depending on you and everything you go through is not by chance. You have to experience truth in order to speak your truth and to be a vessel for someone else. The present and future Kings and Queens are waiting on you to show them the way. You have to be okay with yourself even though you had to hurt and suffer, all of it was for the greater good. It had to happen, and when you see the future flourish, you will then see that it was well worth it.

The hardest poem I've had to write
Taking a moment to reflect on my life
Failures, gains, and growing pains
The poor decisions I've made
Opened up my heart and nearly bled to death
Hurting others with harsh words
Self-hurt I never let go of
Self-hate for procrastinating
Fear that housed alongside my purpose
Hating those that abandoned me

Becoming so angry and filled with rage
Pushing those away who loved me and wanted the best for me
Abba telling me to let go but I held on
Deliberately turning my back on HIM
When I wanted to give up being a mother
Feeling alone and too weak to go on
Not knowing how to mend the broken pieces
Worried about what I didn't have
Being ashamed of who I was
Insecurities eating me alive
The torment.
Allowing fear to defeat me for years
Generational curses I embraced
I can go on and on
I look back at the necessary that had to happen
Taking a deep breath and smiling genuinely
I made it through the darkest hours
Fought with everything I am to make it to shore
Swimming in the deepest seas filled with foreign creatures
Afraid yet doing it anyway, a courageous woman
Conquering so many obstacles that people have died from
Persevering through the hardest and coldest winters
I remained afloat
The blood covered me
It was my safety
God's mercy protected my soul
I floated to safety from the plane crash that should have killed me
Choking on the water
I paddled with all of my might to shore
To get to them
They need me
Hearing the cries
The future
They opened the door through my eyes
Encouragement to reach shore
I finally land on my feet
They become one with the sand
I stand

I walk to dry land into the everlasting safe haven
Tears filling my eyes
I smile
I begin to breathe slowly yet gently
I survived
As their embrace surrounds me
I realize all that was endured was to help save them
To become the relatable instrument
My transparency will heal their today demons
A true hero
I stop and turn around
Looking back at the disaster
My life choices
Things I couldn't control
What tried to pull me down to the ocean floor
To sleep in a watery grave
I say my final goodbyes
Walking towards internal forgiveness as God waits for me
Arms wide open, embracing me with endless love
No judgment, no chastisement, no past, just Abba and I
I forgive myself
I press on towards the sunset called purpose
Carving my eternity
I acknowledge the assignment
I am finally free
I forgive me

Epilogue

No matter your origin, know that you are and will always be a rose in the gardens of torment and demise.
It may try to break, prick, and bend you
Yet a rose will still be a rose.
Beautiful and potent among the ashes of life
So many lonely flowers yearn to blossom but must go through the blooming phase.
As we continually enter the four seasons, know that each season in life will teach a lesson.
It is what you do with that lesson that gives birth to who you are to become.
The choices you make create the life you make.
Acknowledging the first phase of my life is only the beginning.
Setting the foundation for what is to come and who I was destined to be.
The magnitude of all I've endured has led up to this point
Victories and failures as I'm now fully equipped
It is bigger than me
Was always bigger than my life alone
The mantle must be carried by the light stands holding up the light of the world
To show God in His purest and raw form
The relationship - creator to creation - is at stake
Appointed a vessel for many souls in need of rescuing
Battle scars turned weapons helping those to safety
I stand eager to share the second phase of my life with you
Being written in black and white as we breathe each breath.
We shall meet again....

About the Author

Maralyn Burae, born Melissa De Jesus, was born and raised in the South Bronx, New York. The third oldest of six children, Maralyn has been performing since the tender age of three. She was raised by her mother, who was a single parent and a domestic violence survivor. Her father was a substance abuser. Maralyn saw things that ignited her passion and drive to want to provide a better life for her family.

Maralyn began her training at Katz Dance School in the Bronx and later on became a scholarship recipient at the Dance Theater of Harlem. She attended numerous school plays and community performances, which helped develop the many gifts that were growing inside of her. One of her well-known roles was as a mother of two children in a community stage play in which she was the youngest actor, in addition to writing her first project at the age of nine. She has performed both acting and dancing from The Apollo to The Producers Club. She is a single parent and a college graduate of Monroe College and currently has her own independent production company, Celestial Entertainment LLC. located in New York City. She directs, produces, and writes and is currently working on projects that cater to minorities.

Celestial Entertainment LLC. NY is an independent production company that focuses on the arts through visual content. It was established April 5, 2015 with its first stage play debut that was created, written, directed, and produced by Maralyn. She debuted a music video called "Don't Shoot," which focuses on police brutality, civil disobedience, racism, and the daily injustices minorities face, which you can view on her YouTube channel and all social media outlets.

www.ingramcontent.com/pod-product-compliance
Lightning Source LLC
Chambersburg PA
CBHW041232240426
43673CB00010B/315